LET THE STONES CRY OUT

LET THE STONES CRY OUT

DOUGLAS WILSON

This book is dedicated to the session of
Christ Church, a true band of brothers.

Canon Press
Moscow, Idaho
canonpress.com

Douglas Wilson, Let the Stones Cry Out © 2021 by Douglas Wilson.

Cover and interior design by James Engerbretson.
Printed in Canada

Unless otherwise indicated, all Scripture quotations are from the Authorized King James Version. Bible quotations marked ESV are from the English Standard Version copyright © 2016 by Crossway Bibles, a division of Good News Publishers. Used by permission. All rights reserved.

ISBN: 978-1-954887-06-0
ISBN: 1-954887-06-X

CONTENTS

SKETCHES FROM THE CHRIST CHURCH PLANS

PREFACE

January 2021
Dear Friends of Christ Church,

As some of you know, we are in the process of building a sanctuary where our congregation can meet in one place, all together. We have the property, we have the architectural drawings, and we have quite a bit of the money. Our long-standing desire has been to build a place to worship God without going into debt to do it, and this has meant that the "pilgrimage phase" of our church's development and growth has been a good forty years or so—meeting in schools and gyms and so on. That said, we are not yet ready to give the order to the bulldozers, but we can certainly see it from here.

Our elders recently authorized us to make this need known to the broader Christian community. We are not practitioners of "hard sell" giving appeals, as you all know, but our thought was that there might be a number of our friends around the country who would be pleased to donate to something like this, and who would be distressed if they found out later that they had missed an opportunity to participate. That said, to echo the words of Paul, every man should only contribute as he has determined in his heart to give, and not a penny more.

A number of years ago, our elders made a commitment that we were not going to break ground on the building itself until we had crossed a threshold of 60% of the needed funds raised (in hand or in receivables), and until we had pledges for 60% of the remainder. If we decide to build the sanctuary first (instead of the temporary solution of building a large fellowship hall that could house us), we are basically 1% shy of that first 60%. We were able to hit that goal because our members here were so diligent in fulfillment of their pledges that most of it moved over to the cash column. But this means that the needed pledges are currently in the neighborhood of 3 million. That is what we are currently looking at. Our deadline for making our decision on which structure we are going to build first is this coming Spring, 2021.

We do not want a "tall steeple" church for the sake of show. We honestly believe that having such a sanctuary will greatly expand our opportunities for ministry, both locally and nationally. We believe that it would be a resource greatly used. If you think the same, we cordially invite you to participate together with us.

There are two things you can do to help us out. The first is if you would like to give, and the second would be if you know of someone who is in a position to give, but who may not have heard of this need. If that is the case, please pass this information on to them.

———

We do not want a "tall steeple" church for the sake of show. We honestly believe that having such a sanctuary will greatly expand our opportunities for ministry, both locally and nationally.

For those who would like to give, this is how to do it. It is possible to donate to our building fund online with a one-time or a recurring gift (christkirk.com/fundraising), and if you would like to pledge a certain amount, that is possible also (pledges@christkirk.com).

Cordially in Christ,

Douglas Wilson

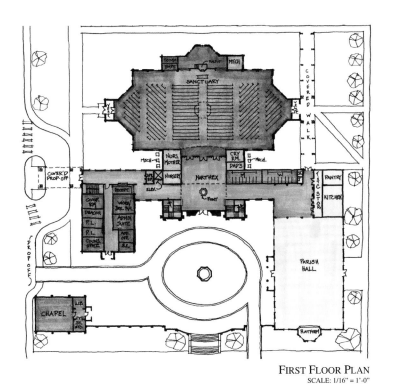

FIRST FLOOR PLAN
SCALE: 1/16" = 1'-0"

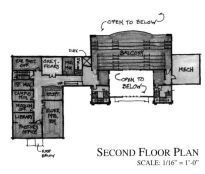

SECOND FLOOR PLAN
SCALE: 1/16" = 1'-0"

CHRIST CHURCH FLOOR PLANS

CHRIST CHURCH SANCTUARY SKETCH

INTRODUCTION

W hen you undertake to build a building, one of the first questions to answer has to do with what the building is *for*. There are times, of course, when a building can be retrofitted to a different purpose than the original architect had in mind, and remodeling can be an enterprise filled with adventures.

Usually the question of purpose is forefront in the minds of the owners and architects. What is this structure for? When the structure is a church, the answer should obviously be that it was built to glorify God. But even this has to be connected to subordinate functions. A church building glorifies God in the architecture itself, but also in how it houses the singing acoustically, and whether it is obvious that preaching occupies a central place, and so forth.

And so we begin by emphasizing some of the basic distinctive that Christ Church has sought to establish in our worship and in our parish life. What are we about? What are we trying to emphasize? This in turn will relate to the kind of edifice that we build.

"Finally, my brethren, rejoice in the Lord. To write the same things to you, to me indeed *is* not grievous, but for you *it is* safe" (Phil. 3:1).

Like every church, the church at Philippi had particular challenges, and Paul addressed them all by urging them to rejoice in those challenges. This is a response that is *always* appropriate because God is always sovereign and God is always good. Not only is it appropriate for Christians to rejoice all the time, it is appropriate to bring to them repeated reminders to do so. To repeat the same exhortations should not be a grief to ministers, and it should be received as a means of keeping us all safe.

But before we repeat the distinctives, we must distinguish two kinds of distinctives. One kind of distinctive arises from what we believe the Scripture teaches and requires of all believers. We focus on it because we believe that all believers should focus on it. This would be a *principled* distinctive, coupled with an ecumenical invitation to all believers everywhere.

A second kind of distinctive would arise from our particular circumstances. These are *tactical* circumstances, tailored to the life and situation of each congregation. Are we in an urban setting or in a small town? Should we build this kind of building or that kind? Should we build a Christian school or is there already a good Christian school? These are tactical questions.

A third kind of distinctive is sinful. This is what happens when a group tries to separate itself from other Christians through various kinds of doctrinal vainglory or ministry showboating. This is what the disciples were arguing about on the road (Mk. 9:34). We are not immune to this temptation (why *would* we be?), and so we want to resist it everywhere we find it. The place to look is under your breastbone.

———

Worshiping God is not a means to another end. Worshiping God is the highest calling that any human being has, or that the entire human race has. It requires no other justification.

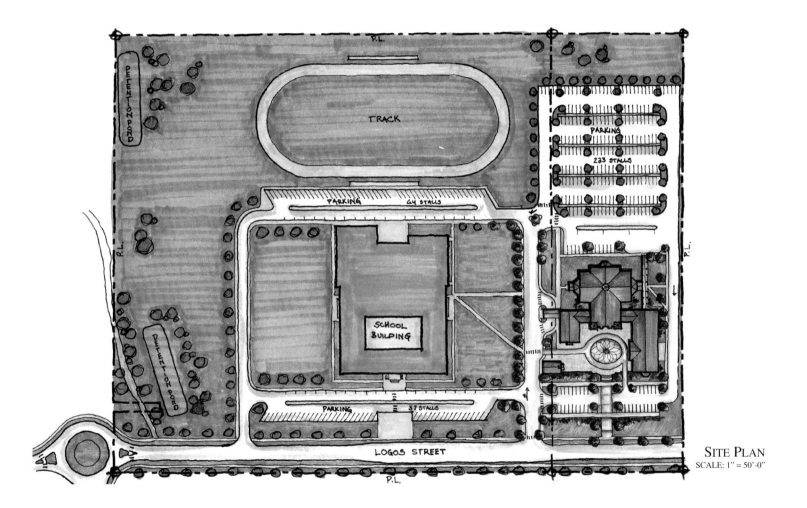

SITE PLAN
SCALE: 1" = 50'-0"

CHRIST CHURCH SITE PLAN

TORO ARCHITECT
WINDOW STUDY
J·Zka·2019

Jesus is Lord, and this means that He is relevant to all things. No area of human endeavor lies outside His authority.

———

That said, what are our principled distinctives?

The first has to do with corporate worship. We worship God because He is *worthy*. We do not do it for any of the results that might come about from it. Rather, we do everything else for the results it might have in helping us to glorify God. "Worthy is the Lamb that was slain to receive power, and riches, and wisdom, and strength, and honour, and glory, and blessing" (Rev. 5:12).

Worshiping God is not a means to another end. Worshiping God is the highest calling that any human being has, or that the entire human race has. It requires no other justification. Whatever we do, it should drive us to this great end. Whatever you do, it should culminate here, in the glorification of God. There is great wisdom in the first question of the Westminster Shorter Catechism here. This is our chief end.

There are of course dangers. One danger is that you make something you *call* worship into a great big deal, but it is not spiritual worship at all. Another danger is that of trying to get worship to "do" other things, like evangelism. But this is backwards.

What are the components of this worship? They would include learning the structure of covenant renewal worship, growing in our musical wisdom and literacy, teaching our families the importance of worship, weekly communion, and practical Bible teaching.

A second distinctive is basic discipleship in community. We want to emphasize basic and foundational issues in our teaching—*personal* piety as measured by *relational* piety (1 John 4:20). We want our doctrine to revolve around practical Christianity, Christian living that is meant to be *lived*. This is why there are recurring themes in the sermons, conferences, books published, and so on. We emphasize things like confession of sin, dealing with bitterness, maintaining relationships, how to read your Bible, the importance of Christian education, and so on.

Any danger here? The danger is the temptation to reduce everything to a moralistic or legalistic approach—to a simple formula. But the biblical approach is always *credenda* before *agenda*.

The components here would include things like: understanding the Apostles' Creed, true Christian education for Christian kids, parish studies, having our lives intertwined in *koinonia* fellowship, and being driven by an eschatological optimism.

And third would be worldview evangelism, outreach, and cultural engagement.

Jesus is Lord, and this means that He is relevant to all things. No area of human endeavor lies outside His authority. Our evangelism is not an attempt to helicopter victims out of a disaster area, but rather is the work of rebuilding a disaster area. Everything is relevant, and everything is related to Jesus.

The Christian faith has cultural ramifications. The Christian faith is political. The Christian faith is public. We have no business taking this light of His and putting it under our own little bushel.

One danger is the obvious one of calling it cultural engagement when we are just drifting along with whatever it is the world is dishing up. Another is the cowardice of shutting up because of the PC police. Or that of using a Jesus stamp on all of your personal prejudices.

The components of this kind of endeavor would include real Christian education (again), and a willingness to get out of our comfy little ghetto. In order to learn cultural engagement, we have to engage. We must not capitulate, and we must not run away. We must *engage*. This means knowing, loving, and praying for non-believers—without trying to become like them.

CHRIST CHURCH SITE SKETCH

xi

CHRIST CHURCH SKETCH

In the coming years, and in the times to come after that, there will no doubt be a number of times when we have practical and tactical decisions to make. A good example would be the issues surrounding the building of our new sanctuary, that we are now on the threshold of doing. We have been without one since this congregation was first established in 1975. We have a church here in town that we planted just fifteen years ago, and which has its own building now, and we still don't, which is the coolest thing in the world.

But when we come to build our own building (or if we do anything else), we need to make sure that everything is brought back to these three areas. How will *this* help us do *that*?

Unless we make a point of doing it this way, we will be like a crotchety bachelor deciding to get married in his late forties. And what could go wrong with that?

The first few chapters of this small book set down some of the basic theological principles involved in building a sanctuary. The remainder of the book is made up of a series of discrete exhortations having to do with the challenge of building, occupying, and using a building—and all to the greater glory of God. Each ends with the same exhortation: Let the stones cry out.

———

Let the stones cry out.

CHRIST CHURCH COLOR SKETCH

1

WHAT MONEY ALWAYS DOES

Our desire is to build a sanctuary that is more conducive to worship than the temporary quarters that God has graciously given us over the years and up to this point. Because we want every aspect of our lives to be governed by Scripture, this means that we must turn to Scripture for guidance and protection as we are preparing to undertake this significant project. When we look at the map that Scripture provides, there are both *zoom out* and *zoom in* features. This section, and the next two after it, are at the *zoom out* level.

"Now, my son, the Lord be with thee; and prosper thou, and build the house of the Lord thy God, as he hath said of thee. Only the Lord give thee wisdom and understanding, and give thee charge concerning Israel, that thou mayest keep the law of the Lord thy God. Then shalt thou prosper, if thou takest heed to fulfil the statutes and judgments which the Lord charged Moses with concerning Israel: be strong, and of good courage; dread not, nor be dismayed. Now, behold, in my trouble I have prepared for the house of the Lord an hundred thousand talents of gold, and a thousand thousand talents of silver; and of brass and iron without weight; for it is in abundance: timber also and stone have I prepared; and thou mayest add thereto. Moreover *there are* workmen with thee in abundance, hewers and workers of stone and timber, and all manner of cunning men for every manner of work. Of the gold, the silver, and the brass, and the iron, *there is* no number. Arise *therefore*, and be doing, and the Lord be with thee" (1 Chron. 22:11-16).

Near the end of his life, King David is entrusting the next big task to his son Solomon. That task was the building of a Temple, and in this passage we see some of the essentials that were involved. The first thing was the charge to build the Temple (v. 11). This was the mission.

David's desire was that God give Solomon wisdom and understanding so that he would keep the law of God (v. 12). The result of keeping this law in wisdom would be prosperity (v. 13), not a truncated legalism. Wisdom and prosperity are given through adherence to the words of God. How could they not be? David then says that in the time of his "trouble," he had nevertheless made a number of preparations for the building of the Temple (v. 14). Not only that, he had assembled the workmen for the task (v. 15). The gold, silver, brass and iron were gathered "without number" (v. 16). Therefore, David said, be "up and doing."

This is the lesson of resources assembled. The principle is that you should take up the hard task of counting your shekels before undertaking the relatively easy task of spending them. Jesus teaches us this principle bluntly. "For which of you, intending to build a tower, sitteth not down first, and counteth the cost, whether he have sufficient to finish it?" (Luke 14:28). Now if your response to this is that Jesus was making something called a "spiritual point" about the cost of

————

The principle is that you should take up the hard task of counting your shekels before undertaking the relatively easy task of spending them.

discipleship, I grant it. But the spiritual point is not one you can grasp if you don't understand the thing Jesus is comparing it to.

You can't afford what you can't afford, and this is something that needs to be determined *first*.

Now David was a king, which meant that he could assemble these riches, and dispose of them the way he does here. He gives these resources to Solomon, and says that *this* is for *that*. He didn't have to route any of this through committees. Our position is different. We are in a much more democratic setting—which has strong and weak points. There are virtues connected to this position of affairs, and there are vices. This means that our financial preparation has to include things like cost estimates, budgets, fundraising, etc. So much is obvious. But another thing we must do—and which I am doing here—is to prepare our hearts to understand money.

We need a big church, and you can't have a big church without big money. But you can't have big money without a big problem, and what is that? Whenever you have big money show up, more than a few people will start acting funny. Sometimes people start acting that way simply because of the *possibility* of big money. This funniness runs in two directions—and we need to learn how to mortify both these tendencies. They are *temptations*. Treat them in just the same way you would treat a temptation to perjure yourself, or commit adultery, or rob banks.

In short, we need to remember that money will do what money always wants to do.

I am not addressing the temptations that people with money face. The warnings of Scripture for them are well-known, and are pretty clear. We do not

———

Whenever you have big money show up, more than a few people will start acting funny.

need to rehearse them here. What we do need to do is go over the temptations faced by people who live in the *proximity* of money. Teaching on this is also found in Scripture, but we are not nearly enough on our guard about it. If someone in our congregation received a windfall inheritance of 100 million dollars, the chances are pretty good that this person would receive *scores* of warnings not to let it go to his head. All the people around that guy will not receive any warnings, and they are the ones who really need it.

They are, respectively, the temptation to be the rich guy's friend and the temptation to be the rich guy's enemy.

The first warning they need is to guard against unctuous flattery. "For neither at any time used we flattering words, as ye know, nor a cloke of covetousness; God is witness" (1 Thess. 2:5).

The second warning is against envious carping. "Thou shalt not covet thy neighbour's house, thou shalt not covet thy neighbour's wife, nor his manservant, nor his maidservant, nor his ox, nor his ass, nor any thing that is thy neighbour's" (Ex. 20:17). "A sound heart is the life of the flesh: but envy the rottenness of the bones" (Prov. 14:30).

Consider a non-monetary illustration. Suppose someone in our congregation, out of the blue, won the Nobel Prize for carving a cure for cancer out of a bar of soap. Next Sunday someone walks up and says, "Congratulations... now don't let it go to your head." He should reply, "Thanks... and don't you get envious." Or someone else walks up, "Congratulations! I always thought you were wonderful! And it turns out you are *really* wonderful! Cousin!" The reply here needs to be more creative.

This is just another way of saying that before we assemble our financial resources to build, we need to take care that we assemble our heart resources. In order for us to handle this great task properly as a congregation, we must learn how to take financial information in *stride*. In order to do this right, we have to practice, practice, and practice.

And, of course, this has everything to do with Jesus.

2

SANCTUARY AS DEACON

A basic truism of modern design is that form follows function. This is self-evidently true, but the reason modern men have found themselves living, working, and worshiping in overgrown shoeboxes is that we have allowed ourselves to drift into a truncated and reductionist view of what our actual function as human beings truly is. Our central purpose, our central task in life, is to worship God in accordance with His Word. The form of a church building must therefore follow *this* function.

"Wherefore laying aside all malice, and all guile, and hypocrisies, and envies, and all evil speakings, as newborn babes, desire the sincere milk of the word, that ye may grow thereby: If so be ye have tasted that the Lord *is* gracious. To whom coming, as unto a living stone, disallowed indeed of men, but chosen of God, and precious, Ye also, as lively stones, are built up a spiritual house, an holy priesthood, to offer up spiritual sacrifices, acceptable to God by Jesus Christ" (1 Pet. 2:1-5).

So, because we are being built up into the new man, growing up into the image of Jesus Christ, certain things must be set aside. If we are to put on the white robe called Jesus, there are certain foul rags that we have to take off in order to do so. We must remove malice (v. 1), deceit (v. 1), and every false front (v. 1). We

The function of a church building is therefore not to be *the church, but rather to* house *the church.*

———

must take away every form of envy (v. 1), which we addressed last week. And if you have a tongue filled with venom, then put that away as well (v. 1). But getting rid of sin, though it is a precondition for growth, is not the same thing *as* growth.

Holiness is not the absence of sin, but rather the presence of something else. We are to be like little babies, who desire the sincere milk of the Word, so that we might grow by it (v. 2). Hunger drives us there in the first place (and this hunger is a sign of life), but then we come back for more because we have tasted it and found that the Lord is experienced as *gracious* (v. 3). We come to the Lord as to a cornerstone that is alive (v. 4). Men rejected Him, but God did not. He is alive, and if we are being built upon that foundation, so are we alive in the same way. We are living stones (v. 5), being built up into a spiritual house and a holy priesthood. We are called to this so that we might offer up spiritual sacrifices, sacrifices that are acceptable to God because of Jesus Christ (v. 5).

The function of a church building is therefore not to *be* the church, but rather to *house* the church. Strictly speaking, the sign out front should not say Christ Church, as though that were the name of the building. Rather, to speak precisely, we should say that "Christ Church meets here." The function of the house is to contain the spiritual house. The function of the church is to provide the church a warm and dry place to compose our worship.

Now the point here is not to be superstitious about word usage, and if someone offers to meet you "at the church," your response ought not to be to rebuke them as a vile transgressor. But we do have to remember that the altar sanctifies the gold and not the other way around.

When the saints start to come in for the service, the building should say, "Shhh . . . the church is here now." The saints should *not* say, "Shhh . . . you're in church now." The building is not God's mausoleum.

This reality is portrayed in Scripture through the figure of a cube. The New Jerusalem that descends down from Heaven is a perfect cube (Rev. 21:10, 16). This is the same shape as the Holy of Holies in the old covenant. The word that Paul uses when telling the Corinthians that they are the Temple of the Holy Spirit (*naos*) is a word that would be used of that inner shrine (1 Cor. 3:16-17; 6:19).

So this inner sanctuary is made up of the people of God. The angel says that he will show John the bride, the wife of the Lamb (Rev. 21:9), and then he shows Him the New Jerusalem. The heavenly Jerusalem is the mother of us all (Gal. 4:26). The New Jerusalem is the place we come to worship every week (Heb. 12:18, 22). *You* are the sanctuary, and you will sanctify the building—not the other way around.

Perhaps it will help us if we think of the church building as an inanimate deacon. Of course we want a church building to do what all buildings do—keep the rain off, and the wind out. But once we have gotten past that basic consideration, what should it do because a *church* meets there?

Peter says that we are to offer spiritual sacrifices, acceptable to God. What are those? What should we offer wherever we might meet, and what could a well-designed building help us do—as distinct from distracting us from doing?

We should therefore consider the elements of a worship service which a building—well-designed and well-used—would help us do. This building is called to be a servant, a tool, an instrument, all employed in the pursuit of that function.

When we come to worship God, here are some of the basic components that a building could help us to do. These are distinct elements of our worship that a poorly designed building would get in the way of, and which a well-designed building would help us with.

First, we *gather*. The word church is the rendering of *ecclesia*, which means "called out." The building should be open and easy to enter.

Second, we gather to *listen* to the Word, and to *partake* of the sacraments. This means we gather in a landscape setting, and not with a long, narrow nave.

Third, we gather in order to *offer our musical praise* to God. The building should sing with us, and not fight us as we try to sing.

Fourth, we gather in order to love one another. The place where we worship should be conducive to a true *koinonia* fellowship.

And fifth, our mission in this community is to declare the crown rights of the Lord Jesus to an unbelieving world. The building from the outside should make that statement in a winsome but authoritative manner.

The building is not ever to become a Jesus substitute. Jesus is our only substitute, and so we want to live in such a way as that when we finally have our sanctuary, we do not find ourselves inundated with those who would attach themselves to a respectable church for all the wrong reasons. There are people who go to respectable churches because it seems like a good place to network with people who might want to buy insurance. But it is not possible to come to a church made of dead stones, but filled with living stones, and not encounter the true and ultimate living stone.

3

LIVING HEADWATERS

Water brings life, and living water more so. We have spoken before on the importance of "assuming the center," and one of the central ways to do this is to create a place from which living water can flow. Water is a *gathering* force.

"Afterward he brought me again unto the door of the house; and, behold, waters issued out from under the threshold of the house eastward... Now when I had returned, behold, at the bank of the river *were* very many trees on the one side and on the other... And by the river upon the bank thereof, on this side and on that side, shall grow all trees for meat, whose leaf shall not fade, neither shall the fruit thereof be consumed: it shall bring forth new fruit according to his months, because their waters they issued out of the sanctuary: and the fruit thereof shall be for meat, and the leaf thereof for medicine" (Ezek. 47:1-12).

In Ezekiel's vision, when the hand of the Lord was upon him (Ezek. 40:1-2), among other things, he saw this: Water flowed out of the house of God, over the threshold (Ezek. 47:1). Water ran out of the Temple on the right side also (v. 2). A man with Ezekiel was measuring it, and thousand cubits out, the water was ankle deep (v. 3). Another thousand and it came to the knees (v. 4). Yet another thousand and the water was waist deep (v. 4). When he went another thousand,

The church is not supposed to function as a rain barrel, or a collection tank. The church is a place from which *the water is supposed to flow* everywhere else.

———

the water was too deep to pass over (v. 5). The man asked Ezekiel if he *saw* that, and then brought him back to the river bank (v. 6). When he got there, he saw that there were many trees there, on both sides of the river (v. 7).

The water will flow east, down to the sea, and heal the waters there (v. 8). Everything will live, wherever that water flows (v. 9). There will be a multitude of fish, and the apostle Peter (with the others) will become fishers of men (v. 10; Mk. 1:17). Even in that glorious day, there will remain some salt marshes (v. 11). Not everyone will be converted, though most will. The trees on both sides of the river will produce abundant fruit, according to month, and watered by the river from the sanctuary, the leaves will be for healing (v. 12).

Now remember from the previous section that the New Jerusalem is the Christian church. We can also see, by comparing text with text, that Ezekiel's Temple is also the Christian church, out of which the living water flows. As we seek to understand this passage, we should begin with this as the key. The key for Christians is always to let the New Testament interpret Old Testament passages, particularly when they are difficult for us. And in the book of Revelation, we are plainly told the meaning of this vision.

"And he shewed me a pure river of water of life, clear as crystal, proceeding out of the throne of God and of the Lamb. In the midst of the street of it, and on either side of the river, was there the tree of life, which bare twelve manner of fruits, and yielded her fruit every month: and the leaves of the tree were for the healing of the nations" (Rev. 22:1-2).

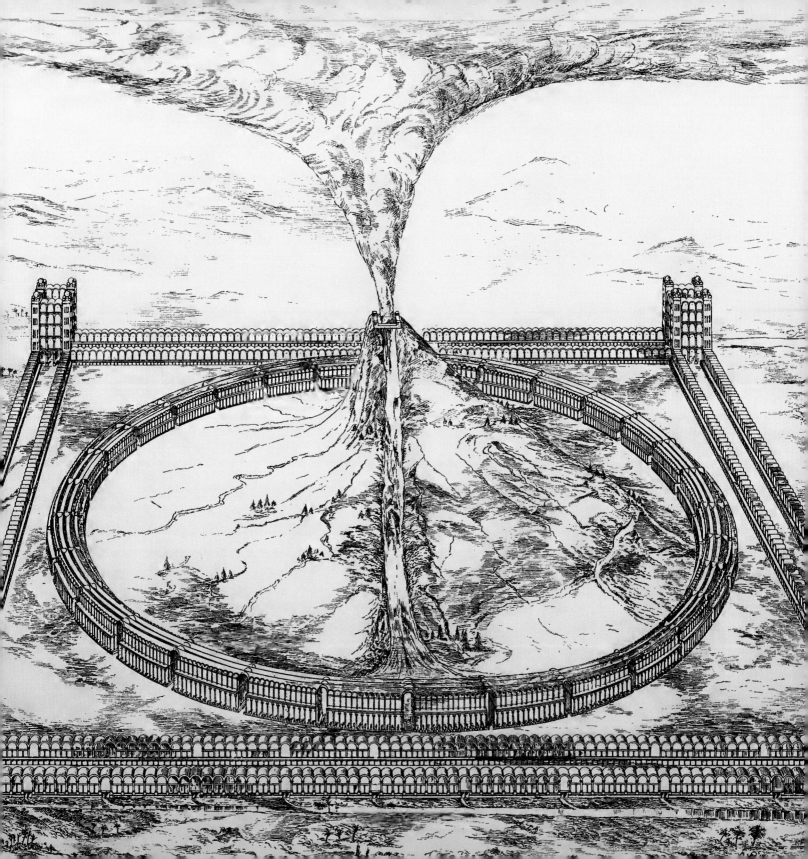

In both cases, we have living water, a flowing river, trees on both sides of the river, monthly fruit, and leaves for healing. So the New Jerusalem is the same thing as Ezekiel's Temple, and both of them are the Christian church. We have a similar picture in microcosm when it comes to the righteous man (Ps. 1:3; Jer. 17:8).

So the church is the place from which this living water flows. Recalling what we saw in the previous section, this living water flows out of *people*. Jesus promises living water to the Samaritan woman at the well, and He was talking about Himself (John 4:11). Whoever drinks of the water that Jesus gives will find that he has become a well of that living water (John 4:14). He drinks and then God makes him a source of living water for others, which is what happens in this instance (John 4:29-30). A few chapters later, Jesus shows how *all* His people become this source of living water. We come to Him and drink because of our thirst (John 7:37), and then living water flows out of us for others (John 7:38). John also tells us in this place what the water is exactly. The water of life is the Holy Spirit (John 7:39). Remember that Jesus said this on the last day of the Feast of Booths, when the Jews had a ceremony of pouring water out at the altar.

"For the Lamb which is in the midst of the throne shall feed them, and shall lead them unto living fountains of waters: and God shall wipe away all tears from their eyes" (Rev. 7:17).

So let us remember the point. So all of this is glorious, but what does it have to do with our pump hou… our new church building? The church is not supposed to function as a rain barrel, or a collection tank. The church is a place *from which* the water is supposed to flow *everywhere else*. The way that the earth will come to be as full of the knowledge of the Lord as the waters cover the sea is because it will flow out of the church (Is. 11:9; Hab. 2:14). Do this, and people will gather to the water.

Having said that, we do not reject intelligent craftsmanship that comes with building particular institutions. So long as we remember the central point, there is no problem with building irrigation ditches, or pumps, hoses, water trucks, channels, canals, or helicopters with buckets below them. Indeed, whenever there are large amounts of water (which we pray for), such things become an absolute necessity. The danger, of course, is to forget what these projects are all for, and then you start to complain about the water—it keeps getting your precious equipment all wet.

Another danger, a great one, is expecting any one building to accomplish what we need to accomplish in our community. But that is like building a rain barrel, and then you are done. No, think of it more like tide pools filling up—first here, then here, then over there.

But when the people of God remember who they are, this mistake is not made. The water flows out of human hearts. The Spirit comes from people, and not from this wooden pulpit, or from that table, or from the bread and wine, or from the baptismal font… or from the building which contains all these God-given activities.

We assume the center when we are filled with the Spirit, and when He flows out of us. The Spirit is the center. This happens using physical things. Spiritual does not just mean like a spirit. Spiritual also means *obedient*. When we offer our bodies rightly, it is our spiritual worship (Rom. 12:1-2). The devil is a spirit who is unspiritual in this sense, and you have ten toes, which can be spiritual—if they are shod with the gospel of peace.

This is because *the living church is always waterfront property*. Many trees grow there, and their leaves have healing properties. The trees grow on both sides of the river, and the river is full of life and brings life. All it has to do is be what it is, and flow. Each one of you is a spigot—and what I want to press upon you is this. Each one of you should walk away from here knowing that you have a critical role in how God is going to cause this water to flow.

———

We assume the center when we are filled with the Spirit, and when He flows out of us.

4

ZEAL

Scripture tells us that we need to speak to our generation with clarity. One of the mistakes that we often make is that of reducing faithfulness in this task to words alone. There are other ways of speaking, and we need to use them all.

Architecture speaks. It is not possible for human beings to live in architectural silence. Because we always want to keep the rain off, we are always speaking. If an alien with anthropological interests were to come and walk through our cities, he would be able tell—without speaking to anyone—what was important to us. He would see business in the skyscrapers. He would see commerce in the great shopping malls. He would see entertainment in the stadiums. And where would he see the importance to us of the worship of the Most High God? We are always

———

Architecture speaks. It is not possible for human beings to live in architectural silence.

speaking… but what are we saying? We are always speaking, but are we speaking the truth?

In other eras, and in some other locations, it has been quite different. Churches were built first, and they were built centrally. They made a statement with their placement, and with their height, and with their architectural *attitude*.

Of course, it should go without saying—although it is safe to keep saying it—that the attitude should be that *God* is great, and is worthy of this statement, not that we are great for worshiping Him in such an admirable fashion. Truly exalted Christian architecture must be both exalted and *humble*.

We acknowledge that such a task is hard, and we are very aware of all the obstacles. Yes, there are many obstacles. But when we have the same kind of zeal for the glory of our Father in Heaven as the worldings have for the glory of Mammon, then perhaps we will do something worthwhile. Building their skyscrapers, and their malls, and their stadiums… was that easy for them? Or are they more dedicated to the worship of false gods than we are in the worship of the true?

So let the stones cry out.

5

PANELED HOUSES

"Is it a time for you yourselves to dwell in your paneled houses, while this house lies in ruins?" (Haggai 1:4).

The first issue has to do with priorities in building. On the safe assumption that we will not have unlimited resources, we want to make sure that when we start in on the building that we give pride of place to those tasks that will enable us to worship God more fittingly. What this means, in blunt terms, is that we want to build a sanctuary first and foremost.

There are other architectural functions that are commonly associated with church buildings that are certainly lawful and appropriate, and we don't want to necessarily preclude such things—fellowship hall, kitchen, office spaces, and so forth.

So if our resources limit us, we want the limitations to land on our conveniences, and not on that which would honor God the most. This is another way of saying that the honor of God should receive the first fruits.

Under our current circumstances, we have offices for the church that are as nice as church offices anywhere. But the task that we say is far more important than, say, the printing of bulletins—the worship of the triune God—is something we conduct in a fieldhouse. When people visit us here in Moscow, we routinely get compliments on how nice the offices are. When they worship with us, I imagine that many of them think, although they are gracious enough not to say, "*Really?*"

Now it is not a sin to worship in a fieldhouse, any more than it is a sin to worship in the catacombs. The Spirit of God is located where His people gather. The worship we offer here is perfect, because we offer it in the name of Jesus.

But what happens when we come down to a choice. Build this or that? Americans are, for both good and ill, a very practical people. This means that we gravitate toward multi-use—"let us do something that, whatever else it does, does not interfere with *our* day-to-day tasks." In contrast to this, we want to make sure that we don't allow such practical considerations—and very lawful considerations—to deter us from honoring God, whatever else we do. So in this next phase of our church's life, we want the honor of God architecturally to be our first and central priority.

So let the stones cry out.

———

So in this next phase of our church's life, we want the honor of God architecturally to be our first and central priority.

6

OWNERSHIP

In order to build a sanctuary in which to worship the Lord, we have to face
the question of *ownership*. One of the reasons why property rights (which are
actually human rights) are under assault in our day is that we have refused to acknowledge that God *owns* absolutely everything. As His creatures, we function as
stewards, under the authority of His Word. If we deny that foundation, then we
will have trouble keeping the house standing.

Now for the church to build a building, we need to own land, and buy
brick and stone, and hire architects, and so forth. This means that we must have
money, and we must have enough of it.

But remember that we are building a house in which to honor *God*. This
means that we must get money from Him in order to return it to Him. We are like
little kids getting money from dad in order to buy him a birthday present. It might
seem like a charade to some, but it really is not. This is one of the deeper and more
profound realities of Christian living. In order to return something to God rightly,
we must get it from Him in the first place.

Now if your father gave you some money to buy him a birthday present,
and you decided to supplement it with money you borrowed from a bunch of
other sources, the chances are pretty good that you will buy him a present that is

more expensive and more tangled up in extraneous obligations than he wanted. It is the same with us.

We don't want to spend a dime more on this project than what God has supplied to us. By the same token, we don't want to spend a dime less than what He has provided. If we do the former, we are entangling our worship of Him unnecessarily. If we do the latter, we are pocketing money for ourselves that He gave us for another use.

In order to be godly stewards of the building the money built, we have to be godly stewards of the money first.

So let the stones cry out.

7

ALL IN

As we marshal our resources, as we count our shekels, we want to remember what the biblical definition of prudence is. We want to be prudent in how we raise money for our sanctuary, but we don't want to be *so* prudent that we are tempted to think we could do something like this apart from God.

God is in the business of doing for His people far beyond what they could ask for or think. But He does this for His people who are walking by faith in the light of His Word. He does not do it for those vain daydreamers who build sky sanctuaries in the clouds.

So the issue is not how much we give. The issue is how much of *us* is contained in what we give. The Lord Jesus commended the widow who put two pennies into the temple treasury, and He commended her because she was obviously "all in."

The reason Ananias and Sapphira were struck down was not because they didn't give enough money. It was because they tried to pretend that their gift was a token of their whole being, and it plainly wasn't. When the widow feeds Elijah with the small amount of meal and oil (1 Kings 17:12), God used it far beyond what she could ask or imagine. The same with the five loaves and two fish. God specializes in this. He loves doing it this way.

When you have a mind to work, the lack of resources is a detail. When you don't have a mind to work, the most trivial obstacle can turn you aside from the way.

———

"Two things have I required of thee; Deny me them not before I die: Remove far from me vanity and lies: Give me neither poverty nor riches; Feed me with food convenient for me: Lest I be full, and deny thee, and say, Who is the Lord? Or lest I be poor, and steal, and take the name of my God in vain" (Prov. 30:7-9).

We don't want to raise so much money that we are building a temple to ourselves. And we don't want to raise so little that we are tempted to connive and manipulate and steal the way many churches have.

So let the stones cry out.

8

THE PEOPLE HAD A MIND TO WORK

We are continuing to meditate on the task of building a sanctuary in our new location. As we do this, we want to make sure we identify all the basic principles that are involved in it. One of them is the nature of work.

Nehemiah once had what could be considered an impossible task, rebuilding the walls of Jerusalem. No sane feasibility committee would have given him the green light on that project. And yet, when the task was operating under the grace of God, what happened?

"So built we the wall; and all the wall was joined together unto the half thereof: *for the people had a mind to work*" (Neh. 4:6).

When God is active, His grace means that work is done. When His grace is absent, then this means that all work turns into tedium and despair. The presence of work is toil, and the absence of work is apathy and hopelessness. But when the people of God are oriented and strengthened by His grace, the results are very different. The people had a mind to work.

When you have a mind to work, the lack of resources is a detail. When you don't have a mind to work, the most trivial obstacle can turn you aside from the way. "There was a lion in the streets," or, "Aliens kidnapped me—what year is it?"

When God gives His people a mind to work, this has the practical effect of readjusting all our priorities. This is not said so that everyone will run and get a shovel—many people who did *not* have a mind to work have been able to go that far. What we want to be doing now is praying for that "mind to work," and we need to be waiting on the Lord for the right moment.

This is said, not so that we might go off half-baked, and then quit early. It is so that we might be preparing ourselves to pray for the moment that He has appointed, and so that it will not catch us by surprise.

So let the stones cry out.

———

When God gives His people a mind to work, this has the practical effect of readjusting all our priorities.

9

DEALING WITH SIN

God hates a particular kind of incongruity with a passion. He detests the notion that we can create a liturgy, or a worship space, or a tall steeple, that somehow masks or deals with sin. But if such things could deal with sin, then Jesus didn't have to die.

"When ye come to appear before me, Who hath required this at your hand, to tread my courts? Bring no more vain oblations; incense is an abomination unto me; The new moons and sabbaths, the calling of assemblies, I cannot away with; It is iniquity, even the solemn meeting. Your new moons and your appoint-

―――――

The world is filled with architectural triumphs that were created because men were trying to deal with guilt.

ed feasts my soul hateth: They are a trouble unto me; I am weary to bear them" (Isaiah 1:12–14).

The night of His betrayal, Jesus was agonizing over what He was about to experience. He prayed that if there was any way to have this cup pass from Him, then *that* is what He would like to do. Nevertheless, He said, whatever the Father willed, that is what He would do. If we could deal with sin architecturally, then the Father turned down Christ needlessly.

The world is filled with architectural triumphs that were created because men were trying to deal with guilt. The results are impressive in one way, but an utter failure in another.

We want to build a sanctuary because we have been *forgiven*, and not in order to commend ourselves to God in order to get forgiveness. We cannot buy the grace of God. We can overflow with the grace of God, and we can testify to the grace of God, and we can rejoice in His mercy by means of brick and stone.

We already know that tormented and driven men can do an awful lot. When we look at the accomplishments of many men, we can almost see the lash behind them. But what can free men and free women do? What can gratitude accomplish?

So let the stones cry out.

10

WORK IT OUT

Whenever we are faced with a challenging or daunting task, there are two problems that can ensnare us. One is when we are very aware of our infirmities, and the other is when we are not aware of our infirmities.

This is how it works. When we are aware of our infirmities, that tends to paralyze us. We are confronted with something we know that we cannot do, and so we do not do it. But if we look at it, and we are swollen in our own conceits, and think that doing it would be a snap, we go on in our own strength and in our own name. That also ends in disaster.

Either our weakness is manifest and paralyzes us, or we are not aware of it, and we proceed under banners flapping in the crisp breeze of our own vanity. When we are paralyzed by the daunting task, we retreat into self-pity—which is what arrogant pride does when it is thwarted. When we are *not* paralyzed by the daunting task, we advance in the glory of our own imagination. We are puffed up—what arrogant pride does when it is not thwarted.

This is why all our labor—which would naturally include the building of a church—must be done to the glory of God. It is not enough to do it all in your own strength, and then put a plaque on the wall in the narthex, glorifying God as some kind of an afterthought. There must be no afterthought about it.

We must do corporately what we are all called to do individually. Paul says that we are to work out our salvation with fear and trembling, for God is at work in us to will and to do for His good pleasure. This is the task—we must work out what God works in, and we must not lay one brick more than that. We must work out what God works in, and so we must lay every brick He gives us.

So let the stones cry out.

———

This is why all our labor—which would naturally include the building of a church— must be done to the glory of God.

11

ARCHITECTURAL CLOTHING

One of the things we need to remember when it comes to church architecture is that a building is corporate clothing. A building is how the whole church dresses. The trick is how to dress up without playing dress ups.

Now we have taught for years that worship ought to be respectful and dignified, not breezy and casual. We do not take out ads in the paper inviting the unchurched to come in their pj's. We are supposed to worship God with reverence and godly fear, and this includes our demeanor, and our demeanor includes our clothing (Heb. 12:28). Paul rejoiced that the worship of the Colossians was in good order (Col. 2:5).

———

The trick is how to keep a stone building from creating stone hearts.

Some of you may have occasionally bumped into me when I am not dressed as I usually am on Sunday morning. The way I usually dress is intended to communicate respect, but dressing this way does not mean disrespect—it only means that the language of respect can vary. But whenever anything is done week after week without ever varying it, the unspoken assumption can take root in a congregation that this is *the* way it is done. And from that to petty liturgical idolatry is just a few short steps. This is even more the case when the dress is explicitly ecclesiastical—robes and so forth.

What does this have to do with a building? If a building is our corporate clothing, and it will be, after we have been worshiping there for fifty years, if the pastor then notices that the congregation has gotten attached in the wrong way, he can't change it up for a week or two in order to make a point. The thing is built out of stone. The trick is how to keep a stone building from creating stone hearts. It is supposed to go the other way. Remember that always.

Living hearts of flesh make the building glorious… and clothing we can use simply as a way of speaking the truth.

So let the stones cry out.

12

NEHUSHTAN MEMORIAL

In Scripture we find two kinds of idols. The first is an alternative to the living God from the get-go. When the children of Israel turned aside to Baal or Molech, they were sinning overtly and rebelliously. They were turning from the living God to false gods.

The other kind of idol starts out innocently. God gave His people something to remember Him by, and at first they remember Him rightly. An example of this would be the bronze serpent that Moses fashioned in the wilderness, so that anyone who had been bitten by a serpent could look on it in faith and live (Num. 21:8). Jesus said that this serpent was given as an Old Testament type, representing His crucifixion (John 3:14). It was a gift of God—and yet, Hezekiah was right to destroy it (2 Kings 18:4).

One of the central things we want to do as we build our church building is keep ourselves from every form of idolatry in and through the process. We don't ever want to be found as having an edifice complex. The last thing in the world we want is to complete the steeple, and find out that the sign outside says Nehushtan Memorial.

So how can we keep ourselves from idolatry in this way? What should we do? The central thing is that our elders must ensure, and our congregation must

insist upon, regular and repeated proclamations from this pulpit, sermons which declare the doctrines of the substitutionary atonement of Jesus, and justification by faith alone.

This can be tricky, as you should see at once, for that is precisely the message that the bronze serpent itself declared, and that did not prevent the children of Israel from burning incense to it. But even the word "tricky" is tricky, because if we repent of our subtleties, it is actually very straightforward. Love God, hate sin. Love God through the blood of Jesus, and hate the sin that He died to remove from you. Live in the justification that His resurrection bought.

So let the stones cry out.

13

SIMPLICITY

As we pray and plan concerning our church building, we want to remember that we worship the God of all beauty. We want the beauty of the Lord to rest upon us as we undertake this task. "And *let the beauty of the Lord our God be upon us*: And establish thou the work of our hands upon us; Yea, the work of our hands establish thou it" (Ps. 90:17).

But biblical aesthetics is not for children, and we must not fall prey to false dichotomies. I have heard, for example, people assuming that beauty should be contrasted with simplicity. But this is fundamentally wrong-headed, because simplicity is a central aesthetic value. Beauty contrasts with ugly, not with simple.

Both with architecture and with liturgy, there are some who assume that "if one's good, two must be better." The liturgy gets cluttered up with bright colors and shiny objects, and the architecture of the church looks, at the end of this process, like a gingerbread architect on acid did the whole thing.

What is beautiful and what we *think* is beautiful are not necessarily the same thing. Our job is to build something of high aesthetic value, but to do so taking into account the fact that the transition between the old covenant and the new represented a basic move in the direction of simplicity and gladness of heart (Acts 2:46).

Those who talk a big aesthetics game are not necessarily good at it, and those who prioritize something else are not necessarily neglecting our responsibility to worship the Lord in the beauty of holiness. And that should be our fundamental realization—real holiness brings real beauty. Sham beauty brings out the tendency that some have to try to glorify God by making the church look like the inside of a circus wagon. On top of that, it is not long before a true sense of the holy and the numinous disappear as well. That whole process leads to churches that become dingy.

So let the stones cry out.

14

CHURCH AS A CHRISTIAN WOMAN

We have already seen that simplicity in worship (and in architecture) cannot be contrasted with beauty, as though it were an alternative to it. Simplicity is an aesthetic trait, and those who think that a building or a liturgy is automatically beautiful because it is complicated, with the maximum number of gold filigrees on it, are not being aesthetically wise. But it is the kind of simplicity that is aesthetically valuable, not laziness.

Simplicity is beautiful when it is elegant. Complexity is beautiful when it is understated. The lines should be clean, not cluttered. Simplicity as an element of beauty is not to be used as a convenient excuse to remain unchallenged, staying with what you are used to. The space we worship in should be *human*, which means that we are simultaneously at home there, and challenged to rise above our current level.

Compare what we are going to do architecturally and liturgically with what a godly woman should do to adorn herself. She should adorn herself, and she should make herself beautiful. But the Bible is explicit that this is not to be done by bedizening oneself with various spangles.

If the church is the bride of Christ, one of the characteristics her adornment should have—as that adornment is architecturally expressed—is the characteristic of *modesty*. When Scripture addresses women about how they should adorn themselves, the consistent refrain is that women should not overdo it (1 Tim. 2:9; 1 Pet. 3:3-5).

As we build, we are adorning. So let us not put the makeup on with a trowel. Let us not assume that more is better, because an adorning simplicity actually says that less is more. In the Book of Revelation, both the New and the Old Jerusalem are adorned. But one is adorned like a bride for her husband, and the other is adorned as a harlot who rides a beast—and she was dressed in purple and scarlet, and was covered in gold, jewels and pearls. The New Jerusalem had her jewels too—but she wore them *differently*.

So let the stones cry out.

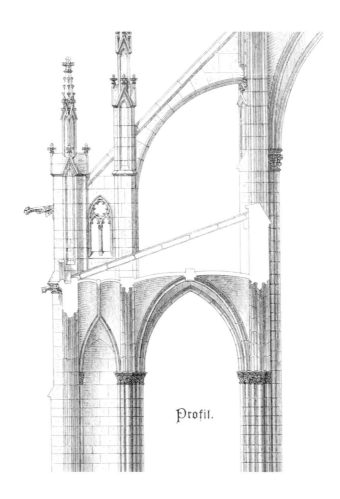

Profil.

15

SIMPLICITY AND SEX

Cultures pass through aesthetic phases as they rise and fall, and the last phase is the phase of decadence. It is the phase in which sensate spectacle is glorified, and it is a sign, not of glory but of decrepitude.

Our generation is currently in the thick of this last phase. Our culture is attracted to the sensational and insists upon spectacle. If you want to see everything that is wrong with our aesthetic understanding, just consider a halftime Super Bowl show, or a Beyoncé concert.

Such things can be impressive, after their fashion. The stadiums filled with people, the logistical expertise that is required, the impressive display that is required, and so on. As we seek to build a building that glorifies God, we obviously don't want it to be a ramshackle affair, but we are also building in a time when people tend to measure beauty by the metric ton.

Another thing should be mentioned as well. This aesthetic decadence is almost always sexualized. As high art tends to be coopted by the homosexuals, so also low art is coopted by the fornicators. It gets to the point where people believe that the sexually pure have nothing whatever to contribute to the arts—they are allegedly the duddy ones, across the board.

But simplicity in architecture and in liturgy are aesthetic values, as I have been urging, but they are also sexual values. When men are given over to the gaudy and gratuitous in one area, you can rest assured that they will soon be wanting to do the same in other areas.

Aesthete and *effete* rhyme, and they rhyme on the spiritual plane also—and for a reason. So when we press for puritan architecture and puritan liturgy, we are doing so for a reason. Reformed theology is not doctrinal content that can fit in any old kind of box. The shape of the gift will determine, over time, the shape of the box.

So let the stones cry out.

16

ACOUSTICAL FAITH

In the beginning, John tells us, was the Word. And the Word was with God, and the Word was God.

We are told other things about the Second Person of the Trinity elsewhere in Scripture—He is the icon of God, He is the wisdom of God, He is the Son of God, He is the light from God, and so on. But there is a peculiar primacy given to the Word. This is that which defines all else.

And this is why, in the Protestant tradition, it is common to have the pulpit in the central position—as a testimony to the centrality of the Word. But it is not enough to give the Word a visual and spatial centrality, and then walk away satisfied, as though our work was done. No, the Word is to have more than symbolic centrality—although it should have that as well.

The Word must have primacy in other ways. The Lord's Table is also central, but it is the Word that makes the sacrament. We are fed at the Table, but the proclamation of the Word is the cooking. The food must be prepared and dressed.

The Word must have primacy because it goes with you in the benediction. I remember a gospel song from when I was a child that said, "I want to be more than a Sunday-go-to-meeting-Christian." The Word is central on the Lord's Day so that the Lord's Day can be the cornerstone of your coming week.

The Word is also central in that it is what is glorified by the music. We are plainly instructed to teach and admonish one another in psalms and hymns and spiritual songs.

And all this is to say that in our new building, acoustics are not just a convenience. Acoustics are not a nice-to-have extra. The attention we pay to acoustics is a testimony to our faith in the centrality of the Word. It will be built as a place where God *speaks* to His people.

So let the stones cry out.

FIG. LXIV.

17

ORANGE STEEPLES

We do not usually have trouble being unselfish about things we don't care about. If something is not connected to us, and is happening on the other side of the world, then the way of renunciation is easy. We let things go quite handily when they are things we never came in contact with.

But when it gets close, and it has the kind of price tag that makes us pay attention, all of a sudden we have *opinions*. These opinions are important, we think, because they are expressed concerning something that is clearly important.

Now it is important to note that there is nothing whatever wrong with having opinions, or offering a perspective. That is what God wants us to do—that is why He gave us our eyes, so that we might see with them. He is not trying to mortify what we see.

But what we need to work on is *how* we see, and how we talk about what we see. Input is great, opinions are valuable, and perspectives are priceless. This is body life. Selfishness wrecks all of it. Selfishness and the pride of ego corrupt what you offer, and makes others (rightly) resistant to what is being offered.

Let us say that the elders decided that they were going to paint the steeple orange, and all the rest of the congregation supported them in this embarrassment. You and your family were the only members who had not lost your minds. The

arguments for doing this were beyond lame—William of Orange; good, hearty Protestant color; and so on.

What you think about this travesty is honored by God. *How* you think about it may or may not be honored by God, depending on how much orange paint we buy, and whether or not it is fluorescent. Remember that being right about the orange won't matter if the steeple of your heart's sanctuary is painted black, with lightning bolts down the sides.

So let the stones cry out.

18

SPEAKING DEFIANCE

The apostle Paul tells Timothy to "fight the good fight of faith." He tells him in the next breath to "lay hold on eternal life." In Ephesians, we are told that our battle is not against flesh and blood, but against principalities and powers. The language of Scripture concerning our pilgrimage here on earth is frequently martial language. It is agonistic.

Our sanctuary, when built, is a sanctuary that is to be used by the church militant. We are not yet in glory, although we ascend to glory every week to worship with the church universal. Nevertheless, we remain bi-locational. Paul wrote to the Ephesian church, which was, obviously, in Ephesus. But they were also in Christ, in the heavenlies. They were located both on earth and in heaven.

This fact is not a respite from our warfare. It is why we are at war. If we were of earth completely, the world would not hate us. The world would own us. But because we represent another kingdom, a kingdom that is coming, and a kingdom that they would all rather have not come, we are a threat, and are treated as such.

The sanctuary is therefore an embassy, an embassy of a rival king and kingdom. As we know, embassies are sometimes honored and respected, although with tension in the air, and other times embassies are assaulted and attacked by rock-throwing mobs.

So when we build this sanctuary, we are not trying to create a little meditative chamber, like the kind of prayer room you might find in a airport. This is a building that should speak *defiance*. There is a certain peacefulness to it, certainly, but in a world full of turmoil, to speak peace *is* to speak defiance. This is because we are speaking peace on God's terms, which means that rebels in arms must lay down their weapons. We do not speak a carnal peace, which can be achieved by dimming the lights and putting a few guttering candles around. We are not playing with the atmospherics; we are building yet another embassy for the kingdom that Jesus is bringing.

So let the stones cry out.

19

ARCHITECTURE SPEAKS

A church building is architectural speech, and so if it is to be a Christian church building it needs to be the gospel in stone. Obviously, it cannot be as specific and defined as a sermon can be, and it does not have symbolic meanings assigned to it by Scripture, as the elements of the sacraments do—water, bread, and wine. But everything in this world speaks, and so we have to take care to speak the truth.

The first step in speaking the truth is to avoid lies, above all, lies that we might want to speak to ourselves. The apostle John says that if we say that we have no sin, we deceive ourselves, and the truth is not in us. This means that a church building needs to declare the glory of God, without veering into the pride of man. The building must not be a monument to ourselves. It must not say, or imply, that we "have no sin."

One of the reasons for building a historic church building is that this enables us to carry all the connotations of Christian proclamation over the last two thousand years. God is great and good, man was created in innocency, we fell from that estate, and God has sent a great Redeemer to save us from our sins by His death and resurrection.

But what we say *about* the building must not be contradicted *by* the building.

It is not a problem that words are necessary to accompany the building, as I am using words now. The sacraments that Christ Himself established work in this way—they require the Word to accompany them. Without the Word there is no sacrament. But the Word fills out the sacrament; it shouldn't fight with the sacrament. The Word tells us that water means cleansing, which would be impossible, for example, if the sacrament contradicted the Word by using mud. In the same way, when we preach the gospel in the new sanctuary, and when we observe the sacraments there, the building must *resonate* with what we are doing.

So let the stones cry out.

20

OPEN CARRY IN WORSHIP

We have noted that a church building is architectural speech. But in order to speak truly as a church, it needs to speak gospel.

Made out of brick, and steel, and wood, and so forth, the architectural vocabulary is limited when it comes to doctrines like propitiation, substitutionary atonement, and so on. The task with such is to avoid speaking of a false propitiation, by building an altar instead of a table, for example. But there is one doctrine of the gospel which architecture can declare very plainly, and without ambiguity.

The gospel declares Jesus Christ as our refuge. The Lord Jesus is our rock. He is our fortress. He is the place of security and deliverance. He shields us. He places us in a high tower. As John Newton put it in his great hymn, "with salvation's walls surrounded, thou mayest smile on all thy foes." A church building can easily speak this kind of security. It is a metaphor, of course, but the transition is a natural one. Every building shelters us from the wind and the rain, but a church building should do it in a way that makes us think of how God shelters us from the world, the flesh, and the devil.

So we worship in a fortress. But the metaphor should never run away with us. This does not mean we should walk around in here like we were an armed garrison—open carry at worship would make a *liturgical* statement, one that we don't want to make. That statement would be that we consider all the others here to be potential enemies, not brothers and sisters. We are in the sanctuary, not in an Old West saloon. Concealed carry is different, and no more a problem than having a church building with a sprinkler system installed in case of fire.

We would not be dubious about open carry at church because we were afraid of guns—far from it. The problem is liturgical, not practical. This is a secure fortress, and so we never want to install our anxieties into the liturgy. *Here* we are foreshadowing the time when we hang the trumpet in the hall, and study war no more (Is. 2:2-6).

So let the stones cry out.

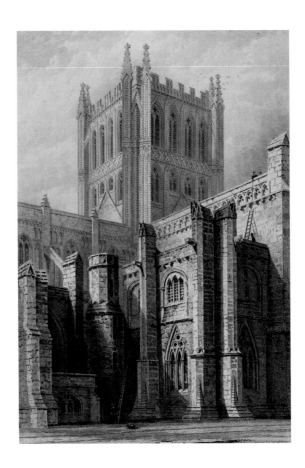

21

THIRD COMMANDMENT

As we continue these short meditations on our new church building, we should reflect for a moment on the name it will have. Our church building will have the name of our church—Christ Church. The name of our church bears or carries the name of our Savior. We never want to take, or bear, or carry, the name of God in vain, so what is involved in that?

In Deuteronomy, the people of God were told to exterminate the Canaanites. This was a God-ordained ethnic cleansing. Particularly they were to go after the idolatrous worship, and note this—and "destroy the names of them out of that place" (Dt. 12:3). But nature abhors a vacuum even here, and this was done so that the name of God might be established in the land (Dt. 12:5). God was going to select a place to put His name.

But great wisdom is required. Centuries later, when Jesus was talking to His disciples about the Temple where God had established His name, He told them bluntly that God was going to level the place (Luke 21:6). And why? Because God cannot endure iniquity and solemn assembly together. When the disciples asked about this, about when this would all happen, Jesus warned them about false teachers—many will come in my *name*, He says (Lk. 21:8).

So then, when we build this place, it will have the name of Jesus Christ attached to it, and in some manner His name will be carved in stone. Do not let that stone be an emblem of the condition of our hearts. We want this to be a place where we earnestly confess our sins, where we are cleansed and forgiven, where we make our oaths and promises, and where we are equipped by the grace of God to keep them. In short, we want our church building to avoid being a violation of the Third Commandment, just as we want it to be an expression of our zeal to fulfill the two greatest commands.

So let the stones cry out.

————

We want our church building to avoid being a violation of the Third Commandment, just as we want it to be an expression of our zeal to fulfill the two greatest commands.

22

INESCAPABLE BUILDING

We have been considering the building of our new sanctuary, and want to make sure that we are evaluating all that we do in the light of God's Word.

One of the first things that men do when they are stirred up is that they build. The building can take various forms—music, and poetry, and so on—but of course one of the obvious ways to build is through buildings. This "stirring up" can be the effect of reformation and revival, or it can be the forces of apostasy. But when men are *moved*, they build.

Apostates and infidels build. That was what we had in the tower of Babel. "Let us make us a *name*," they said, but the upshot was that the Lord gave them the name Babel (Gen. 11:4). Nebuchadnezzar looked out at the splendor of Babylon, and there, on the very precipice of insanity, said "is not this great Babylon, that I have built?" (Dan. 4:30). God made man upright, but man has sought out many inventions (Ecc. 7:29). Not only does he invent them, he builds them.

But it would be a great mistake to think that the ungodly build, and that the godly do not. The distinction is found in what we build, and how we build it, not whether we build. So we built the wall, Nehemiah says, because the people had a mind to work (Neh. 4:6). In the reformation under Josiah, the Temple was restored (2 Kings 22:5). When the Spirit moves among God's people, they start to build. This is because we are imitating Him, and He is building us. We are living stones. We are His workmanship, created in Christ Jesus to be doing the work we are doing.

So it is not whether we build, but rather what we build and why. Why should we build anything? Because the Spirit is at work in us. What should we build? We should build tools that enable us to do what God placed us in this world to do. The first thing, the central thing, is the worship of God. That is the work we were created to do, and all the other work we do flows out of that.

So let the stones cry out.

———

We should build tools that enable us to do what God placed us in this world to do. The first thing, the central thing, is the worship of God.

23

GRATITUDE

One of the common sins that the people of God in Scripture commit is the sin of forgetting God's deliverances and mercies. And one of the great reasons for forgetting His mercies is the fact that we continue to enjoy them.

When God delivered His people from Egypt, after they were out of Egypt they didn't have to deal with it anymore. In the wilderness, this meant that they remembered Egypt falsely, which is to say fondly, and once they were in the land of promise, Egypt became a distant memory—something that ancestors went through in the history books. And when we change the curriculum, we forget all about it.

So ironically, ongoing mercies make us forget the establishment of those mercies. As we are considering the building of a church sanctuary, we want the building to remind us of God's kindness to us, and not to be a new environment which we can take as our birthright, as just the way things are, as just the way this congregation rolls.

The key is gratitude, gratitude that is expressed and not just dialed in. We know how to dial it in. We all know, for example, how to say grace at the beginning of meals. That is something we just do, and wouldn't dream of not doing. But suppose the head of the home stopped the meal in the middle, and told everybody that the food was really, really good, and why don't we say grace for a second time? That would seem odd, weird, contrived, and perhaps… more grateful. It would highlight how the initial grace we say is sometimes said on cruise control.

When we have our new building, we do not ever want our gratitude for it to go on cruise control. We want to be constantly thankful, and to be fresh in that gratitude. The way to do this is to be a people who are thankful every day for the sun coming up, for the milk in the fridge, for the grass in your lawn, for the forgiveness of sin.

So let the stones cry out.

24

THE SOLID HOUSE

T he house of God is a great house, an expansive house. We refer of course to the Church of God—as the promises of God have established her, spread out through all human history. As we look in faith to our brothers and sisters, we see portions of that great house, but we see it through a glass dimly.

When we build physical structures, we are should be reminding ourselves of the same realities, looking for the city whose maker and builder is God. The church building is not the Church, but church buildings do speak about the Church. But just as writing in a book is no good to someone who does not know how to read, so also the gospel in stone is of no use to the one without evangelical faith. What is evangelical faith? It is spiritual *literacy*. The natural man does not understand the things of the spirit because they are spiritually discerned. But the spiritual man knows and understands what God is saying, even when He says it in church architecture.

Paul speaks of surety of the foundation of God. The NKJV renders it as a *solid* foundation.

"Nevertheless the foundation of God standeth sure, having this seal, The Lord knoweth them that are his. And, let every one that nameth the name of Christ depart from iniquity. But in a great house there are not only vessels of gold and of silver, but also of wood and of earth; and some to honour, and some to dishonour" (2 Tim. 2:19–20).

Just remember that when we have built a solid church, one you can touch, this is simply a type of the great house, the final church, the ultimate city. But do not forget that the one that is coming is far more solid, more real, *more* tangible, than what we will be able to build. And as the stones represent the living stones that will rejoice in the presence of God forever, so let those who would be living stones depart from iniquity.

So let the stones cry out.

25

THE FURNITURE OF GOD

When God has His people undertake a building, it is *not* so that He might have an empty box dedicated to Him. Under the older covenant, even the holiest place of all contained *furniture*—the ark of the covenant with two great cherubim overarching the mercy seat. And the placement of that furniture meant a great deal—in that Holy of Holies, the law of God was kept inside the ark, but under the mercy seat. And so that is how we treasure our commitment to the law—under the mercy.

In the new covenant, the house of God contains three great items of furniture, and all three of them are gathering points for the people of God. The building itself is where the church, the *ecclesia*, the called-out ones, gather or assemble. We are an assembly, but we are an assembly that has gathered in accordance with Scripture. We as God's people are the church, but the furniture represents the reason for the church.

In chronological order, the central items of furniture a church should have are these—a font for baptisms, a pulpit for declaring the Word of God, and a Table so that the people of God might commune with their God. Now of course it should be perfectly obviously that these are simply tools that testify to God's ordinances, saying *amen* to what the Scripture says about them. Baptisms can be performed at the river, without a font. Sermons can be preached from a tree stump, and often have been. The people of God can commune with bread and wine in hidden places, where tables wouldn't fit. The furniture is not essential, although the faithful testimony of what they contain is always essential.

So to the extent that we are building at all, we should want the building to say what the Bible says to say. Baptism says that our sins are washed away. The Word of God gives shape and direction to our lives. The bread and wine nourish us, giving us strength to do as we have been directed. And we build in accordance with that.

So let the stones cry out.

26

EVANGELISM

A church building is a staging area, designed for God's people to use in fulfilling the mission. The mission is the evangelization of the world—for the universal church—and the evangelization of our locale, for the local church. As a staging area, we have to be able to see past it. Marshaling and assembling the troops is not the same thing as sending them out to battle.

This means that if we build our building, and within a year or so it is not big enough to contain us all, that is not a sign of poor planning. It is a sign to us that we are beginning to accomplish the mission. Our goal should not be to have a sanctuary big enough to hold us all, so that we might then settle into our long, slow glide plane into cultural irrelevance.

Moscow is a small town, but we nevertheless want our great-grandchildren to have a choice of ten solid Reformed churches, each with their own building. Not only that, but because we are postmillennialists, we would like to see those Reformed churches not at war with each other.

The Great Commission was to disciple the nations, and so our marching orders here on the Palouse are to disciple the Palouse. Church growth must not be thought of as a zero sum game, where one church can only grow at the expense of the others. No, not at all. Christians churches are built out of former non-Christians. Our task is evangelism and discipleship. Our task is birth and growth. Our task is to see our region of the country fill up with the knowledge of God.

Church buildings are a tool that can help us do that. They can also be a distraction, where possession of the tool becomes the thing instead of using the tool. We should not be like the children of Israel who invaded the land of Canaan with sufficient force to remain there themselves, but not sufficient force to displace them… and their idols.

So let the stones cry out.

27

WHAT REMAINS

Scripture tells us to strengthen the things that remain—strengthen the things that appear to have some lingering stability. Shore up the permanent things.

But because of our penchant for idolatry, we sometimes make a grave mistake when it comes to this. We see churches and cathedrals built centuries ago, and we think that the stone and brick are what remain because they are still here. But those who built these structures from a vibrant and true faith are now with God, where they will live forever. They remain, while the world and everything in it do not. The grass withers, the flower fades, but the Word of the Lord is forever.

The faith of the people is the *soul* of the building. The building itself, without living, evangelical faith—without songs pouring out of forgiven hearts, without a proclamation of truth that is piping hot, without prayers of honest and sincere contrition—becomes a mausoleum. When the people are alive, the sanctuary is animated and alive.

Nothing true will ever die. No sincere sacrifice to God has ever gone extinct. We strengthen the things that remain so that they will continue to remain, and this is all by the grace of the God who has said that whatever work He begins, He will complete.

The Holy Spirit does not build the kingdom in fits and starts. His work is purposive, all of it. Everything has a function. He does what He does in accordance with the counsel of His will. Some tools are used up in the course of His work—like a building—while other things grow increasingly useful—like you.

We are not the scaffolding for the building; the building is the scaffolding for the true church, the church that will stand forever. To the extent that the dead stones are a help to the living stones, we rejoice in their use. If they get in the way, it would be better to meet in places like rented gyms until the Lord comes.

So let the stones cry out.

28

GENEROSITY

James tells us that if we sin at just one point of the law, we are guilty of offending against all of it. This is because the law is simply a description of what the triune personal God is like, and so an offense against Him at *this* point or at *that* point is still, at the end of the day, an offense against Him. If a man were to strike another man, whether the blow falls on his right cheek or his left, the blow has still fallen on the *man*.

Now the point of our sanctification is to become like God. That is where we are going. If we forget this, as professing Christians, what happens is that we find ourselves keeping a bunch of detached rules, and forgetting what the person behind all the rules is actually like. What He is like is love, kindness, overflow, and everlasting generosity. The detached rules may be fine in themselves, but when we do this they are radically out of context. By keeping just some of the rules we got from God, we do it in such a way as to sin against God.

When we seek to accumulate enough money to build the sanctuary we are pursuing, we need to accumulate it through generosity, not through hoarding. A church is a conduit for ministry, and it is—in line with the character of God—a replicating ministry. This means that we must be *constantly* putting seed in the ground. "Now he that ministereth seed to the sower both minister bread for your food, *and multiply your seed sown*, and increase the fruits of your righteousness;) Being enriched in every thing to all bountifulness, which causeth through us thanksgiving to God" (2 Cor. 9:10–11). *That* is what we are after.

Now there is a counterfeit generosity that just throws resources this way and that. When the prodigal son was buying drinks for the house, he was *not* imitating the character of God. But when his father had the stalled calf killed for the welcome home party, and hired a hot little jazz band for that party, he *was* providing us with an image of the character of God. But upon returning home, did the returning prodigal really need to go to another *party*? Well, apparently Jesus thought so.

So a building campaign is not a time for us to put ministry, generosity, open-handedness, and so forth, on hold. It is not a time for us to temporarily become tightwads, so that we may be better prepared to overflow in true open-handedness a number of years from now. That's not how it works, and that is not what happens.

So let the stones cry out.

––––

When we seek to accumulate enough money to build the sanctuary we are pursuing, we need to accumulate it through generosity, not through hoarding.

29

CONFESSION AND CONSTRUCTION

When Nehemiah heard about the desolate state of the ruined city of Jerusalem, he was greatly humbled, and he cried out to the Lord in true confession of sin.

"We have dealt very corruptly against thee, and have not kept the commandments, nor the statutes, nor the judgments, which thou commandedst thy servant Moses" (Neh. 1:7).

This was the man who was to rebuild that city, and so he began by clearing the spiritual ground—he began with confession of sin.

Just as every attempt at true godliness in our day-to-day lives should begin with confession, and just as every worship service begins with confession of sin, so also any project as large as building a city, or a temple, or a Christian sanctuary should begin with confession of sin. If God were to mark iniquities, no one could stand, and so there is always something to confess. In short, we can confess the reasons it has not been completed by now.

Now all great building projects are built on blood, on a foundational murder, and it is no different here. Where there is not true faith, the foundational murder is like Cain's slaying of Abel before he built his city, or it could be like Hiel the Bethelite rebuilding Jericho (1 Kings 16:34). But for believers there is only one

way to deal with sin, and only one way to build anything. For us the foundational murder is not hidden away, nor has it put on a dark veil. We are able to build because our hands and hearts are clean, and they are clean because they have been washed in blood.

We are building a sanctuary that will be dedicated to the worship of God, but it will not contain blood sacrifices. It will not be built *with* any blood sacrifices. This is because all the builders have been cleansed by the once-for-all sacrifice of Christ, who is the cornerstone for every faithful work—including this work.

So let the stones cry out.

———

We are able to build because our hands and hearts are clean, and they are clean because they have been washed in blood.

BIRTH AND GROWTH

The task of the church is the evangelization of the world, and to bring that converted world up to maturity in Christ. The task of the local church is to do its part in that global task in its part of the world. Notice how the apostle Paul described his mission. "Whom we preach, warning every man, and teaching every man in all wisdom; that we may present every man perfect in Christ Jesus" (Col. 1:28). If the point of the world is for humanity to grow up into the perfect man, then the point of every part of the world is to grow up into its portion of that perfect man. Global evangelization is therefore the sum total of the faithful labor of local churches. The global community will not be evangelized by the global church—it will be brought to Christ by the ministries of local churches.

And this means that local churches must think of their mission differently. We are not here to gather a tiny portion of the population in order that we might take a small splinter of humanity off to Heaven. No, we want to bring Heaven here. In line with how we pray in the Lord's Prayer, we want His kingdom to come, not go. We want His will to be done here as it is already done in Heaven.

The task of the church here on the Palouse is therefore *birth* and *growth*. We are called to be constantly engaged in the evangelism of unbelievers, and once they have been converted and baptized, we want them to grow up to maturity in

Christ. Our task is not that of isolation and containment. Now in order to bring the Palouse to Christ, it should be obvious that we are going to need something that human beings need for everything else that they do—we are going to need buildings. And if we are going to need buildings, it is self-evident that we are going to have to build them. But in the building of them, we must take care that we not become distracted by them. They are a resource to be used and expended in fulfillment of the mission—birth and growth.

So let the stones cry out.

Reculver Church, Kent

CHALLENGES

Everyone in the world thinks he understands. That is what it means to think. In order to think, you have to think something. And whatever it is that you think, that is what you think.

So if you are in the grip of an error, you do not understand that error. If you did, you wouldn't be in error. Who can understand his errors? When Scripture poses this question, it poses a profound question.

Understanding error, and understanding the truth that stands opposite from it must therefore be a gift of God. Apart from grace, there is no way to comprehend what is happening in the culture around us, in the church at large, in our own congregation, in our own families, or in our own hearts. But when God's grace is poured out, the people are woven together in like-mindedness, and the people have a mind to work.

Many churches are not aware of their fundamental disunity because they don't have to work on anything *challenging* together. The standard operations of the congregation are on cruise control, and so simmering discontents don't really affect anything much. But when they undertake a large project, like building a sanctuary, they discover that before you build a church, you need to have built the *church*.

Only a true church can build a church building in a way that glorifies and builds up the true church. When the work is done, the congregation should be closer, tighter, more committed to one another, than they had ever been before. As the bricks go together, sealed and set, the bricklayers should be even closer.

The stress of a challenge tests everything. It brings selfishness to the forefront, and it brings love and consideration to the forefront. So never forget, in the course of construction, we are building the invisible things first, and the visible things are designed to be simply a wonderful echo of them.

So let the stones cry out.

———

The stress of a challenge tests everything. It brings selfishness to the forefront, and it brings love and consideration to the forefront.

32

SANCTUARY AS WINDOW

We are physical creatures, living in a physical world. At the same time, God has put eternity in our hearts, which means that we are enabled to look beyond what is merely physical. Because we are material creatures, God always works with us through means. Because we are spiritual creatures with an immaterial soul that is not bound or limited by mere matter, we are enabled to know what those means *mean*.

Those who look to the means alone, stopping there, are superstitious and blind. They think Jesus is the bread and wine. They think salvation is the sinner's prayer. They think that God dwells in houses made with human hands.

Those who look to the meaning alone, bypassing the means that God has established in the world, are gnostics and rationalists. They are too spiritual to be confined to physical things. They think that Jesus does nothing in and through the bread and wine. They think salvation means looking down with contempt on the sinner's prayer. They think that God dwells in the bone box on top of their body.

But the man who is given a true, spiritual understanding approaches God through His appointed means, knowing that the material creation is a window through which we are called to see God. It is not a mural of God, and it is not

God itself. Neither are we on the other side of the window, able to apprehend God directly.

Focus on the sacraments and you are an idolater. Focus on the externals of a gospel presentation straight out of the book of Romans alone, and you are an idolater. Build a church building that functions as a mausoleum for a dead god, and you are an idolater. Throw away the sacraments, and the Bible, and places for meeting, and you are the worst idolater of all—thinking that *your* ego by itself might be able to ascend to the sides of the north. So our church sanctuary will have windows, of course. But it will also *be* a window for the faithful.

So let the stones cry out.

———

So our church sanctuary will have windows, of course. But it will also be *a window for the faithful.*

33

STEEPLES OF PRIDE

All of this is submitted to God, but, Lord willing, our church sanctuary is going to have a steeple. And a steeple illustrates the perennial problem that believers have in this fallen world. A steeple can be illustrative of the humility of man before God, but it can also be a glaring example of the pride of man. We want the former, but the latter is never far away.

One the one hand, we know how small we are before God. A steeple expresses the finite yearning of creatures for the transcendent, and it points to the only place our salvation can come from—from Heaven above. This is a God-given humility. On the other hand, in the course of building it, we might come to notice that it is taller than those *other* steeples, and that the design is more fitting. This kind of thing can even reach pathological levels, where we take pride in how much more humbly we yearn for the transcendent than they do.

Pride is an insidious sin, and it is capable of working with *any* materials. Human pride can glory in having no steeple at all, and we could all worship in a tiny little box calling one another by the names of *brother* and *sister*, greeting each other with the phrases like *grace and peace*, and a holy kiss, sprinkling our conversation with words like *yea* and *verily*, with the women vying with each other over who had the plainest bonnet, and only be doing any of it because we thought we were *better*.

Can a beautiful woman take pride in her makeup? Well, certainly, but pride doesn't go down the sink as easily as the makeup does. The only thing that deals with the pride of life is the gospel of Jesus Christ, with application of that gospel being made by the Holy Spirit of the Father, who straightens things out where it all begins, which is in the human heart.

So what do we want our steeple to mean? Among other things, we want it to be a summons to the prideful. We want it tall so that the purblind can see it. This is the place where we all of us must come to die.

So let the stones cry out.

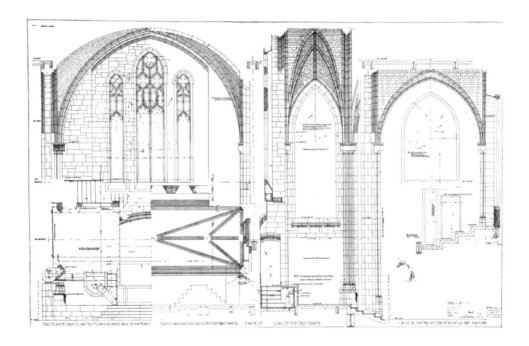

34

ANGLING FOR RESPECTABILITY

A building speaks of permanence. So when we build a church building—especially if there is a lot of brick and stone involved—this speaks of permanence as well. But we have to be careful. For Christians, this material world is not the final state of things. However, this does not mean that the final state of things will be ethereal, or spooky, or wispy, or spiritual in any of those senses.

The solidity of a church building speaks of the ultimate solidity of the new creation, when matter will receive its final glorification in the resurrection, and when atoms will be packed together far more densely than they are now. Your salvation, and the salvation of all God's people, is far more *real* than anything you have ever experienced up to this point.

A church building speaks of this by *analogy*. A spiritual dullard takes the enacted metaphor literally, and thinks that ultimate reality is found in what we have done, what we have fashioned, what we have made. But the privilege we have in this world is to yearn for the next. The whole creation groans, Paul tells us, longing for the time the sons of God are to be revealed. That groaning creation includes everything we build, including the sanctuary.

The best way to ensure that our building continues to speak the truth about the next world is to make sure it stands against all that is false in this one.

The system of the world is wrapped up in the lust of the flesh, the lust of the eyes and the pride of life. Our spire, our sanctuary, our windows, should all be fashioned as an *obstacle* to those who would find their satisfactions under the sun. In our day, this means that want to build what we build as a testimony against the secular state. We want it to be an eloquent testimony, but that means there will be temptations that come with it—temptations to pretend to be against something we are secretly working for. The answer is, of course, the blood of Jesus, which what this sanctuary must always proclaim. There is no way to preach the gospel and angle for respectability at the same time.

So let the stones cry out.

35

ICHABOD MEMORIAL

When Solomon dedicated the Temple, one of the things that happened is that the glory of God filled the Temple, such that the priests could not even go in (2 Chron. 7:1-2). When Moses communed with the Lord at the door of the tabernacle, God appeared there in a pillar of glory (Ex. 33:9). When Jesus was transfigured on the mountain, He together with Peter, James, and John were enveloped by a bright cloud of glory (Matt. 17:5).

Now it is important to remember this because we are seeking to build a church building that speaks of the glory of God, and we want it to speak about glory truthfully. I say this because glory is not something that fossilizes. When the Spirit departs, the glory departs, and the church building becomes Ichabod Memorial.

What will protect us? How will God deliver us? This is a folly that has ensnared many. Our preservation is in the name of the Lord, and the name of the Lord is only revealed through the gospel. The name of the Lord is revealed through the folly of preaching Christ crucified. We declare that God was in Christ, reconciling the world to Himself, and that Jesus, the God/man lived a perfect and sinless human life, on our behalf, and that He was slain on a cross, and His blood ran down. When His blood ran down, it was for the cleansing of all His people, and, good to His Word, after He rose from the dead, He applied that blood—your only hope—to the great altar in the heavenlies. And from that place, He prays for you, and He prays for you by name. He prays for *this* congregation, by name. Our task is to echo His prayers, which is what it means to pray in His name.

So let us always glory in that gospel. Let us never exchange the glory of God for a fog of nuance. When Christians get nice things, like a building, they frequently get above themselves. The folly of God is wiser than men, and so our task is always to follow His folly, and not our own wisdom. And that means the cross.

So let the stones cry out.

PLATE 4

36

HONESTY

In his great psalm of confession, the psalmist says that he has acknowledged his sin to God, and then goes on to say that he had not hidden his iniquity (Ps. 32:5). Because we live in a world full of sin, and because we as God's people live our lives here, when we come to church one of two things must happen. Either we will come to understand our sin and deal with it properly, or we will come here to hide it.

Hospitals are institutions dedicated to health, but they are not places where we go to enjoy and celebrate how healthy we are. You do not go to the doctor in order to lie to him about all your symptoms. What would be the point?

The assembly of the church is a similar kind of thing. We want to come here for a genuine encounter with God, and this means that we must not come here in order to hide our iniquity. He knows about it already. He knows far more about us and our issues than we do. He knows everything there is to know about it. He knows when we come to church and do not confess our sins honestly at the beginning of the service. He knows when we move through the rest of the service pretending that we didn't track in what He knows we tracked in.

When we do this kind of thing, we demonstrate that we are not really worshiping God, but rather are worshiping the good opinion of our fellows.

And this is why our steeple is going to have a cross on top of it. We erect that symbol because we want our town to know, and we want to constantly remind ourselves, that we have been called to a life of virtue *by grace*. And because it is virtue by grace, the foundational virtue that the grace of God cultivates in us is honesty. And that is how this building needs to be built—as a refuge for the honest.

So let the stones cry out.

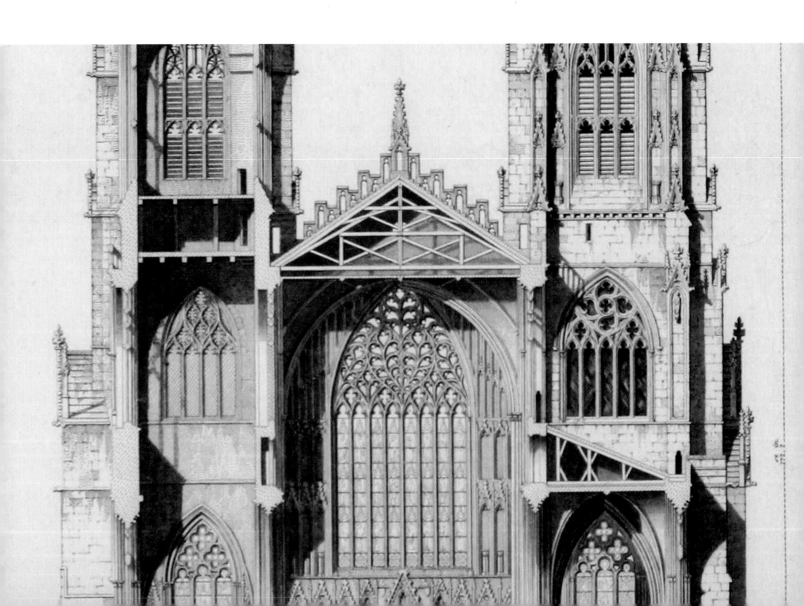

37

KEEP ON KEEPING ON

When God established His church in the first century, there were a number of unique things about it. The surrounding world was overwhelmingly pagan, and so the burgeoning Christian movement had to make certain decisions about priorities. The first thing that happened after Pentecost was not a building campaign. Neither was it a political movement. The initial explosion of conversions was followed by a century or more of evangelism. The Christians met in all kinds of *ad hoc* circumstances. The catacombs are justly famous, but the New Testament also records multiple times how believers would met for worship in homes (e.g. Col. 4:15).

By the second century, the number of Christians was much greater, and almost from the beginning they challenged the pagan establishment on a number of issues. The Christians were adamantly pro-life, and rebuked the pagan tolerance of abortion and infanticide. If you want paganism without an attendant contempt for life at the margins, you want something that has never existed. The Christians modeled a different approach to compassion during plagues and epidemics, shaming the pagans by their compassion for others. The Christians also opposed the gladiatorial games. Killjoys from the very beginning.

The same kind of thing happened with church buildings. We did not build the great structure of living stones because we had all these attractive brick and mortar buildings. It was the other way around. Life, community, fellowship, love, discipline, care for one another, are all the ways you build the *actual* church. When you have done that, it is time to move on and make an institutional declaration, one that challenges the principalities and powers. But if we are not doing it from homes, and gyms, and open air meetings, we are not going to do it when we have a nice, respectable place. When we get a nice sanctuary, we must always remember what got us to that place—and keep on doing it.

So let the stones cry out.

38

GOD'S ARTIFACT

Pride is a protean thing, a true shape shifter. Whenever a creature desires to believe in his own superiority, this is a desire that can be projected onto *anything*. When it comes to the erection of buildings and sanctuaries, we can take aesthetic pride in the beauty of what we have done, or economic pride in the efficiency of what we have done, or moralistic pride in the humility of what we have done, and so on down the line.

But the problem with pride is the *pride* part, not the accomplishment part.

God put us into the world to accomplish things, and we are to be grateful to Him when He enables us to do these things. But when we veer off into pride, we can take pride in having done what God gave us to do, or we can take pride in doing something else instead. The problem is the heart attitude, always.

When we have built something, the pride of man wants to look out over it all, like Nebuchadnezzar on the walls of Babylon, and somehow to take credit. This is the beginning of insanity—it might come suddenly, as it did with Nebuchadnezzar, or it might creep up slowly, as it has for many others.

We want two things therefore. We want God to prosper the work of our hands, and we want Him to keep reminding us that even our hands themselves are his handiwork. We have been saved by grace through faith, and not by works, to

97

head off the boasting. At the same time, while thwarting every carnal boast, God has created us as His workmanship, His artifact, to do good works, which He prepared beforehand for us to do. So as we build let us remember that we are being built, and all of it by grace.

So let the stones cry out.

39

THE ACTUAL INCONSISTENCY

God tells us in His Word that as His people we are to come out from the world, and to be separate from it. This separation, this distinction, is what holiness means. To be holy is to be set apart.

The fundamental point of holiness is to have God make a distinction in His people between righteous living, and lives of corruption. "Wherefore come out from among them, and be ye separate, saith the Lord, and touch not the unclean thing; and I will receive you" (2 Cor. 6:17).

We can also make something holy by setting it apart from common use—we wouldn't use a communion tray as a cake platter at a church potluck, for example. But even this kind of thing is simply an audio-visual help, enabling us to understand the difference between sin and righteousness. David ate the show-bread, and it would be lawful and right for us to use the communion trays in some sort of comparable emergency.

Just as the altar sanctifies the gold, and not the other way around, so also, the physical accoutrements of worship are sanctified by our *actual* worship, proceeding from our actual realization of a humble and contrite heart. All of this applies most forcefully, most centrally, when we are contemplating the construction of a sanctuary.

We want a place that reminds us of the inconsistency between a house of worship Sunday morning, and a time of loose living Saturday night. That loose living can take many forms—raunchy movies, corrupt friends, ungodly parties, envious snark and complaining, and all the rest of that unsightly crew. So when our sanctuary is built, we want you to come into it prepared to reason in a "how much more" fashion. As this place seems inconsistent with the movie I watched last night, how much more is it inconsistent with the presence of Christ's Holy Spirit in my heart, hands, mouth, and life?

So let the stones cry out.

40

GIFT ON THE ALTAR

Most Christians appreciate the blessings of actually having a church building, but many Christians also detest many aspects of getting the buildings built. Chief among the objects of our distaste would be the vexed problem of fundraising. This is not surprising, because it is too often the case that we want to pursue a Holy Ghost mission with the devil's funding model.

The Bible does tell us that God loves a cheerful giver (2 Cor. 9:7), but it does no good to harangue everybody with this glorious truth if the leadership of the church insists on doubling down on all the things that make cheerful giving impossible. So in the conviction that a godly approach to funding is not going to happen by accident, we are going to spend some time in considering what the Bible teaches about righteous giving. This will only happen if God preserves the imagination of the thoughts of our hearts.

"I know also, my God, that thou triest the heart, and hast pleasure in uprightness. As for me, in the uprightness of mine heart I have willingly offered all these things: and now have I seen with joy thy people, which are present here, to offer willingly unto thee. O Lord God of Abraham, Isaac, and of Israel, our fathers, keep this for ever in the imagination of the thoughts of the heart of thy people, and prepare their heart unto thee" (1 Chron. 29:17–18).

Drawn by the late T. Hearne, after the fall of the West end in 1806.   Engraved by Ja. Redaway

Leave your gift right where it is, and go arrange payments with your brother first.

————

So let us begin with the conditions under which we may *not* give to our building fund. You cannot love God, whom you have not seen, if you do not love your brother, whom you have not paid.

For some mysterious reason, Christians frequently take Christ's instruction about leaving our gift at the altar as a prohibition of taking communion if your brother has something against you (Matt. 5:23-24). Perhaps there is something a little self-serving in churches letting the people think this, because Jesus is actually prohibiting giving a fat donation to the *church* when there are issues between you and your brother.

Now frequently such issues between brothers are financial. Sad to say, brothers frequently flake on brothers. Sometimes it is for twenty cents and other times it is for 20 grand. So if you have any outstanding obligations—for work promised, for payments unfulfilled, whatever it was—stay out of our fundraising campaign until that is all cleared up. And if you have an acute conscience for all those instances where people have flaked on you, but have a half-inch callus on your heart with regard to all the bags you have left others holding, then that means you also are not qualified to give to the new sanctuary. You may *not*. Leave your gift right where it is, and go arrange payments with your brother first.

So let the stones cry out.

41

TRIBUTE TITHE

Whatever we do, we should seek to do it all to the glory of God. This includes the details of our worship service, certainly, but it also includes other issues, like architecture and design. But a step behind that is the question of money, and raising money. Underneath all of it is the heart attitude of God's people, wanting to do what God wants us to do, and doing it the way He wants us to do it.

When it comes to money, we have already noted that you should refrain from giving to the church if your financial affairs are not in order. If your brother has a beef with you—and such things are frequently financial—leave your gift un-presented until things are good between you and your brother. If God doesn't want it, then why give it?

But there are other financial aspects to all of this. Do not give convulsively, in the emotional heat of a building campaign. Labor instead to become a tither, one who consistently gives ten percent of your increase to the Lord's work, as He leads you. You might think that a group of non-tithers would have more money available to give in a spasm of giving, but this is not the way it works. In a God-honoring campaign, disciplined givers can do a lot more by giving a little more than usual, than undisciplined givers can do by giving what they think is a lot.

We want the church sanctuary to be a center of grace, a center of giving, a place from which blessings *flow*. The building is an emblem of the people themselves, and we want to be a people who pay tribute to God. That is what the tithe is, actually. We do not give ten percent so that God will leave us alone with our ninety percent. That would just be an ecclesiastical extortion racket. Rather we give ten percent as tribute, a ten percent that says in a very tangible way that one hundred percent belongs to God. And it does not really matter how much of it there is. What matters is what percentage of it is *blessed*.

So let the stones cry out.

42

THE BOX IN THE BACK

I n the matter of giving and receiving, the church has responsibilities, just as the giver does. We have seen that God wants His people to refrain from giving financially when there are unresolved conflicts in the church. We have also seen that giving is a response of obedience over time, and not the result of an emotional warp spasm. But what responsibility does the church have?

The first is that the church is responsible to be teaching the people the "whole counsel of God" (Acts 20:27). We are not to teach what the Bible says in bits and pieces, but rather are to gather it all up in a systematic whole. But this includes teaching the people what the church should do in the presence of the people, and not just what the people should do for the church.

When it comes to godly fundraising, there are two basic methods employed in the Bible. When Paul puts the godly squeeze on the saints, it is for the sake of distributing practical relief to others (2 Cor. 9:2-4). Even there, there is a point made of having accountability (2 Cor. 8:18-20), but Paul does lean on the saints to dig deep and give… to the poor.

When it comes to building construction or reconstruction, the method we see in Scripture is the method of putting a box at the entry way of the sanctuary. This is how the Temple was rebuilt under Jehoash.

"But Jehoiada the priest took a chest, and bored a hole in the lid of it, and set it beside the altar, on the right side as one cometh into the house of the Lord: and the priests that kept the door put therein all the money that was brought into the house of the Lord" (2 Kings 12:9).

We also see that this is how donations were taken in at the Temple at the time of Jesus. The Lord watched as the widow woman put her two mites into the offering box at the entry to the Temple (Mark 12:42).

This is why, incidentally, we don't pass the plate during the worship service. We *present* our tithes and offerings as part of our worship, but we don't collect them that way. When we pass anything around, it is to distribute, to give. When we celebrate the Supper together, the elders send men out into the congregation to give, not to take. And when the Lord leads *you* to give, you may do so at the entry, and with no one looking over your shoulder.

So let the stones cry out.

43

WASTED ON GOD?

I t is obvious that building a sanctuary takes a lot of money, and compared to what most families handle in the course of their operations, it takes a lot of it. At some point in the preparations or building, it is therefore likely that someone will ask whether or not this expenditure is "wasteful."

Though it may seem prudent and wise, it is actually the logic of Judas. "Then saith one of his disciples, Judas Iscariot, Simon's son, which should betray him, Why was not this ointment sold for three hundred pence, and given to the poor?" (John 12:4–5). The short form is that if it is not somehow being spent on us, or in ways that we can directly benefit from, it is being wasted. If it is spent on glorifying *God*, we tend to think we are pouring water into sand.

How about a multi-purpose building? That way we could give God *His* gift, and we could use it too. Kind of like a time-share tithe.

Now there are obvious ways in which we could pretend to glorify God while not actually doing so. If we built a sanctuary out in the wilderness that we visited once every fifty years—that would not be a good use of resources. But we want to build a sanctuary is used regularly and constantly, and in the advancement of God's kingdom.

This will include evangelism, and benevolence, and other ways of reaching out to our unbelieving community. But beauty lifted up to Heaven is not an adjunct to what we are called to do; it is the very center of what we are called to do. Worship of God is no afterthought. A visual statement of God's heavenly authority, an acoustic space that enables us to praise Him in glory, a place on earth set apart to indicate our ongoing obligations to true worship of the true God—these are not throw away items.

So the use of money to accomplish such things is something that pleases God. He does not want us to adopt the hard logic of the pragmatic Judas. He wants us to lift our eyes to higher things, and money is simply a tool for helping us do this.

So let the stones cry out.

44

WHY?

Why have a church building? What is the point? What are we trying to do with it?

The first reason is one that sanctuaries share with all buildings whatever. That reason is the wind, snow, rain, and so on. God has put us in a world where we require shelter in order to do the things that God has called us to do. Even foxes have holes, and birds have nests, as the Lord pointed out (Matt. 8:20), and we are creatures also.

The second reason has to do with the opportunity to glorify God. We are not the only creatures who build shelters, but we *are* the only creatures who talk by means of them. We are the only creatures who decorate them. From stadiums to skyscrapers, man uses brick and concrete and r-bar to speak. For churches, we ought to use these things to preach.

The third reason is that a building—used rightly—becomes a staging area, an organizational point for all the things the church is called to do during the course of the week. In our case, this would include evangelism and outreach, college ministry, benevolence, and so forth.

And fourth, a building is a casing, a receptacle, to house God's people doing what God commanded us centrally to do. What is that? We are told to gather weekly, to hear Scripture read, to sing psalms and hymns, to hear the Word of God proclaimed, and to break bread together. We are supposed to get together in order to love one another.

Last, we build because we are human beings. When human beings are stirred up, the first thing that happens is building. When the Spirit moves among His people, He motivates them to shape the world in a particular way, and to have that shape acquire something of a permanent form. If we do not do this, it means that we have not been stirred, we are not moved. But that is not the case here.

So let the stones cry out.

45

FUNDRAISING AND FAITH

Another aspect of funding a church building is the important element of faith. We often feel like we are supposed to trust God for "spiritual" things, like our salvation, but that when it comes to finances we have to learn how to be "realistic." Unfortunately, being realistic often means adopting worldly techniques that could just as easily be used in building a civic auditorium.

But God's people need to do everything differently. And even when we do something externally similar to what unbelievers might do, the insides of the thing have to be totally differently. Jesus says this about how God cares for us.

"Consider the lilies how they grow: they toil not, they spin not; and yet I say unto you, that Solomon in all his glory was not arrayed like one of these. If then God so clothe the grass, which is to day in the field, and to morrow is cast into the oven; how much more will he clothe you, O ye of little faith?" (Luke 12:27–28).

The admonition at the tail end of this says it all. "O ye of little faith" means that we need to learn how to trust the Lord who loves to adorn things. This is a "how much more' argument, and Jesus says that we are to look at the flowers of the field and reason from that to what God has prepared for your wardrobe. And we are therefore invited to reason from both the flowers of the field and your

wardrobe to the way our sanctuary will look and feel when we are done.

Men without faith build things too, and the results of their work are either sterile or excessively gaudy. This is another way of saying that a true and living faith has a lively aesthetic sense.

This means that we must take care to make sure that faith is our motivation in every aspect of this, from the fundraising to the placement of the cross on the steeple.

So let the stones cry out.

46

EMBLEM OR MASK

As we pay attention to our Christian lives, as wve ought to do, we have a tendency to focus on the things we do or have done, as though the whole thing were a matter of bookkeeping in a ledger, instead of taking our actions as indicators or "tells" of what we are turning into. We are either growing up into the perfect man, the Lord Jesus, or we are growing in a slow spiral toward some tragic and very lonesome finality. But the mercy, or the justice, as the case may be, are examples of transformation, not examples of an arbitrary sentencing falling on very similar creatures.

When congregations build church buildings, this is either a testimony or a mask. It is either a declaration of what we are all becoming in Jesus Christ, or it is an attempt to substitute with blocks of stone what God will only receive from tender hearts.

If the latter is the case, it would be far better to forego building altogether, and just concentrate of getting our hearts right. Neither do we want to be okay with God at the start but have the challenges of building become a point of stumbling. We know how it is possible for someone to be so frazzled by wedding prep that they are in no spiritual shape to enjoy the wedding. Or a woman preparing a celebratory meal to be so overwhelmed by the work that something quite distinct from celebration is being prepared in her heart.

Scripture says this: "Better is a dry morsel, and quietness therewith, than an house full of sacrifices with strife" (Prov. 17:1). In the same way, it would be far better to worship in a gym forever than to build a glorious building that functioned as a wrecking ball for the actual spiritual building, the one made out of living stones.

Fortunately, it is not necessary to choose. But we should always know, *if* we had to choose, what that choice would be.

So let the stones cry out.

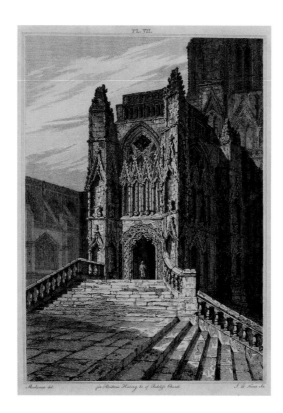

47

GOD'S SUPPLY

Hudson Taylor once said that God's work done in God's way will not lack for God's supply. What this means is that we, if we are walking in the will of God, are never short. We always have the resources for doing what we are supposed to be doing at that moment. If we don't have the resources for going forward, we have the resources for waiting. If we are supposed to go forward, we will have the resources to do so. And mixed in with this is the teaching of Scripture that sometimes we are to step out in faith. We are to go forward in response to God's leading, and the resources will meet us at a pre-appointed rendezvous.

Open your mouth and I will fill it, God says. On the mount of the Lord it will be provided. There are times when we have to trust for the resources, but we do this in accordance with the teaching of Scripture, and the examples found throughout Scripture.

Wisdom is called for. We are not to run ahead of the Lord, willfully seizing what we think *He* has for us. We must be directed and steered by the Lord. But it should be equally obvious that God doesn't steer parked cars. If there is no motion, it doesn't matter how much the steering wheel is turned back and forth.

God has prepared certain good works beforehand for us to do (Eph. 2:10). This is not just true of us as individuals, or for our families. It also applies to congregations. As we are called to the building of a sanctuary, we must approach that work, and the preparation for it, as in the fundraising, with a spirit of confidence. If this is something God has called us to, then nothing on earth can stop it. And if it were not something God called us to, then He will thwart it, but we didn't want it anyway. Remaining in the will of God should never be a disappointment.

So let the stones cry out.

48

CELEBRITY CHEFS

Architecture needs to be, like all other forms of human expression, honest. There must be no pretense, no sham, no attempts at misdirection. Centrally, when we are talking about the architecture of a church, the honesty must be of the kind that plainly recognizes that God is God, and we are not.

When you come into a church to pray, it must be the kind of place that helps you tell the truth, instead of the kind of place that aids and abets in the telling of lies.

There are many examples, but here is just one. It is easy for a traditional church with a very long nave to tell all the people that God is distant, down there at the other end. This is not said in so many words, but it *is* said. And we acknowledge that God is transcendent, utterly beyond us, but in Christ through the gospel, He is the God who is with us, who has come down to us, who is present with us in our assembly. And this is why our seating is in a landscape layout, and not a portrait layout.

Picture the people of God gathering together around the Word and sacrament, the way we would gather around anything that was of great interest to us. This is an architectural expression of what we believe the church is. The church *is* an assembly of saints—not a long line of supplicants, where you have to stand in the back craning your neck.

And in this, we do not set the Word and sacrament into competition with each other. The service is not a zero-sum game, where the sacrament must give way to the Word or vice versa. Word and sacrament go together the way cooking and eating do. Services with great preaching and no sacrament are like celebrity chef television shows, where a lot of good food is prepared but not eaten. And sacramentalists are the ecclesiastical equivalent of a raw foods movement, where you come to church to get your puny carrot.

So let the stones cry out.

———

The service is not a zero-sum game, where the sacrament must give way to the Word or vice versa. Word and sacrament go together the way cooking and eating do.

49

TESTIMONY

The people of God are the congregation of testimony. We worship and serve the God who intervenes in human history, and we are among those who testify to what He has done. We are to do this with our lives, with our families, and with our collective and corporate worship. We testify, and we are to testify in all that we do. This includes whatever sanctuary we might build. Is the testimony true? If there is no true testimony, there is no true sanctuary.

The ark of the covenant was called the ark of the *testimony* numerous times (e.g. Ex. 26:34). The two tables of the Ten Commandments were called the "tables of *testimony*" (Ex. 31:18). The tabernacle was called the "tabernacle of *testimony*" (Num. 1:53). Our task is always to testify to God's testimony, re-

―――

If He has no testimony concerning us, then we can have no testimony concerning Him.

sponding to it faithfully. God says "I have acted here," and we say "Yes, He did." And remember that when we seek to build a testimony, there will be those who don't want us to—like Sanballat and Nehemiah's wall.

The philosophers Hume and Kant, in a frenzy of high conceit, helped to banish "testimony" from the modern world as a reliable source of knowledge. We want an idolatrous way of knowing that what we *think* is indubitable. But we are finite, and so it has to be testimony or nothing. Jesus is Lord, so it is *testify and live* or *languish and die*.

What do we testify to? We testify to the presence of Jesus. The Lord your God is in the midst of you. Jesus is under your breastbone, and throughout the congregation. *That* is what we are talking about.

"The Lord thy God *in the midst of thee* is mighty; He will save, he will rejoice over thee with joy; He will rest in his love, he will joy over thee with singing" (Zeph. 3:17).

Our testimony is based upon receiving God's testimony. *He* testifies, and we either believe Him or we do not. Jesus came from Heaven and testified (John 3:31). "And what he hath seen and heard, that he testifieth; and no man receiveth his testimony. He that hath received his testimony hath set to his seal that God is true" (John 3:32-33).

Not to believe Jesus is to call Him a liar. And here in 1 John we have this glorious statement:

"He that believeth on the Son of God hath the witness [*marturia*] in himself: he that believeth not God hath made him a liar; because he believeth not the record [*marturia*] that God gave of his Son" (1 John 5:10).

So what then is true testimony? In order for us to have the right kind of testimony, we have to know that it is *God's* testimony. If He has no testimony concerning us, then we can have no testimony concerning Him. We are echoing the story of what He has done, and when we tell the story of what He has done, He is continuing to do it. We tell our testimony faithfully when we are *keeping* His testimony (Ps. 119:88).

So let the stones cry out.

50

REVERENCE

One of the central things that a place dedicated to worship should do is frame a space that is conducive to true worship, and to do so in a way that does not tend to draw "worship" to itself.

With regard to the first, we have to ask ourselves what a Christian worship service should be like. Contrary to the operating assumption of many Christians today, it should not be a breezy and informal affair.

First, worship should be disciplined and orderly, as Paul commends the Colossians for having just such a worship service. "For though I be absent in the flesh, yet am I with you in the spirit, joying and *beholding your order*, and the stedfastness of your faith in Christ" (Col. 2:5). Not only must it be orderly, it should be attended with reverence and godly fear. "Wherefore we receiving a kingdom which cannot be moved, let us have grace, whereby we may serve God acceptably with reverence and godly fear" (Heb. 12:28). The word rendered serve here is *worship*. This means that when churches strive to create a sense of casual informality, they are striving to do the wrong thing.

But the second task of a worship space is also important. In one sense the worship space is set aside for the congregation, and the congregation is the bride of Christ, formed as such by the Holy Spirit. One of the distinctive characteristics of the Spirit is that He draws attention to the Son, who brings us to the Father. The Spirit is not garnering attention for Himself, and neither should a sanctuary do so.

So if a worship space goes overboard in giving "too much" glory to God, the failure is seen in how the glory does not take you on to the actual worship of God. And this failure, of course, is not actually a case of too much glory to God, which is impossible, but rather a mistaken attempt to render the wrong kind of glory to Him, which winds up giving glory to the creature instead.

So let the stones cry out.

51

HOPE DEFERRED AND THE TREE OF LIFE

The gospel gathers us, and our subsequent worship consists of what we *say* and what we *enact*. We say, we confess, that Jesus is Lord and we believe in our hearts that God raised Him from the dead. But Jesus said that if we love Him we will do what He said, and the very last thing he said for us to do is disciple the nations, baptize them, and teach them to obey all that He commanded. There it is—our marching orders: *disciple*, *baptize*, and *teach*. Pretty straightforward.

We are doing this in a world full of physical people who have immortal souls. In order to speak to their souls, we have to send bodies. We enact what we believe, with words, with water, with bread and wine, and with brick and mortar. In order to reach people who live in this world, we have to establish patterns of true worship in every place on this globe, and we have to do this in a way that does not interfere with the genius of the mission.

If we deliberately build a sanctuary that is just a glorified big box store, then we are fighting our own message that Christ is the embodiment of all that is true, good, and beautiful. But if we worship God in catacombs or field houses because we have the long view, and know that God's strength is made perfect in weakness, then everything is quite different. As one historian put it, the Christian church lives in the light of eternity and can afford to be patient. Patience is a virtue, and is one of the characteristics that the Spirit establishes in our lives.

But as true as that is, it is also true that God has placed us in time, in history, and we should want to *see* the progress of the gospel we live for. "Hope deferred maketh the heart sick: But when the desire cometh, it is a tree of life" (Prov. 13:12). This applies to evangelism, to Bible translation, to book publications, to church planting, and to the occupation of sanctuaries.

So let the stones cry out.

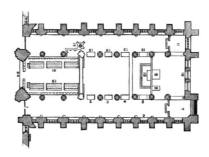

52

WINESKINS

As we are preparing for a sanctuary of our own, we have to remember that we are not the only ones doing the preparing. Not only are we preparing in all the ways we know about, so also God is preparing us—in many ways we don't usually know about.

When denominations form, and when church buildings are built or occupied, what we are seeing is the institutionalization of the church. This is not a bad thing—it is necessary in the very nature of the case—but it can easily become a bad thing if we are not being prepared by the Spirit of God to take our place in wisdom.

There is nothing that can be done to keep new wineskins from becoming old wineskins. If you have a new wineskin in time and in history at all it will at some point be an old wineskin. That is the role of the much disparaged "institutional church." The institutional church is the wineskin. There are temptations that come with this, sure enough, but you can't opt out of that temptation by rejecting wineskins generally. Something must hold the wine, and so if you go the airy fairy route, pretending to have no wineskins at all, you are either kidding yourself or just hastening the time when you have wine all over the floor.

New wine is any work of the Spirit of God in the midst of His people at the beginning of the process of fermentation. Fermentation is the process of becoming potent, and it involves much change and activity. Such fermentation is what we would call reformation and revival. When God energizes His people, and does a great work in their midst, they can frequently find themselves in conflict with the "institutional church." We need to remember that it was the leaders of God's people who had Jesus crucified, and we also need to remember that Jesus spoke far more roughly to the rabbinical theologians than he did to demons or the devil himself.

So as we see our wineskin taking shape, we want it to be much more like Nicodemus—hungry for the approaching work of God—than like Caiaphas, who was entirely hostile to the approaching work of God. So as we are praying about the institution *we* are preparing for, we want to pray that we will have anticipated and prepared for the fermentation. We want to install vents.

So let the stones cry out.

53

A DUDDY-DEAD ONE

Biblical wisdom literature often encourages us to prefer one of two offered paths, when there are actually four possibilities. For example, we are told that it is better to have a little money and fear of the Lord than to have lots of wealth and big trouble with it (Prov. 15:16). We are also told that thin soup and thick love is better than a sumptuous meal and hatred around the table (Prov. 15:17). It is better to be humble and with the lowly than to divide the spoil with the proud (Prov. 16:19).

The old gospel hymn frames it this way: "I'd rather have Jesus than silver or gold." And this is very much a biblical way of thinking. But remember there are actually four possibilities. 1. You could not have Jesus and not have silver or gold. 2. You could not have Jesus and have silver or gold. 3. You could have Jesus and no silver or gold. 4. You could have Jesus *and* silver or gold.

Now it is the point of the wisdom comparison to make us realize that this fourth option is not nearly as easy as it looks. It was wealth and the cares of this world that choked out the crop in the parable. This is why Jesus warned about camels and the eye of the needle.

This said, it would be better to have a vibrant church that meets in a gym than to have a duddy-dead one meeting in an architectural glory. We say this, not because we are limiting ourselves to these two options, with only one righteous choice. We must always recall that there are four options, and two righteous choices. But at the same time, we are instructed to think this way so that we keep our priorities exactly where they ought to be.

It is relatively easy to keep these priorities now, because we are in a gym. But a certain kind of theology and preaching will dictate a certain kind of sanctuary, and this is healthy. When we get that sanctuary, we need to remember that the sanctuary will start to demand a certain kind of theology and preaching, and that will not be so healthy.

So let the stones cry out.

54

CHOICE TRIANGLE

One of the things our elders learned from our architect is what might be called a choice triangle. For any new construction, there are three basic elements to the project. Take the square footage, take the quality of design and materials, and take the dollar amount to be spent. Those are the three corners of your triangle. As you look at those three elements, you may pick any two, and the two you pick will determine the third for you.

If you have *this* amount of money and no more, and you want *this* square footage, then that will determine the quality of construction. If you want *this* quality of construction, and to spend *this* amount of money, that will determine how big it is going to be. You get the picture.

The two you pick determine your priorities, and the one that remains for you is the cost you must pay for your priorities. If costs must be limited, but high quality is essential, then the cost you must pay is in size. Any one of the three of them can be the cost you pay, and any two of them can represent your priorities.

As we look to build a sanctuary, our task is to seek to have our priorities reflect God's priorities, and God's task is provide in the third area. This is because we usually bump up against a cost for our standards that is a cost we do not want to pay. That is where we seek the Lord for provision. So we have certain architectural standards, and good for us. Are those standards biblically grounded, biblically responsible, historically informed, and theologically aware?

In other words, in the two areas we pick, are we being biblically responsible, such that it is not presumption when we look to the Lord to provide for us in the third category? Hudson Taylor once said that God's work done God's way will not lack for God's supply. The psalmist said that God promises us this—open your mouth and I will fill it. But that opening must be in true and intelligent faith.

So let the stones cry out.

55

PRESUMPTION AND TIMIDITY

W hen undertaking the construction of anything, but particularly a sanctuary, it is important to balance two things. The first thing is that you do not want to be presumptuous about the future. The second is that you must walk in faith, in full confidence about the future. If you are reading the story you are in, then you should be anticipating how the next chapter is supposed to go.

With regard to the first, the Bible is very plain. You do not know what tomorrow will bring. Our lives are a mist, a vapor, a bit of cloud in the mountains (Jas. 4:14). Why then do we make confident pronouncements as though the future were held by us? To behave this way is presumption.

So what is faith? To a secular observer standing off to the side, faith can *look* an awful lot like presumption. "Now faith is the substance of things hoped for, the evidence of things not seen" (Heb. 11:1).

On the one hand, you don't want to run on out ahead, writing faith checks on the assumption that something magic is going to happen in your bank account if only you write the checks fast enough. On the other hand, playing it safe—burying the talent in the ground—is not safe either. It appears that God wants us to avoid two kinds of foolhardiness—one that is rash and the other that is timid.

Suppose we build a sanctuary for a thousand people and a thousand people don't come? Suppose we overshoot like that? Suppose we set our sights low, build a much smaller sanctuary, and God says "so be it according to your faith," and we have trouble filling *that* one? What if this and what if that? Better yet— what if we trust God?

One of the names the Bible has for us is *believers*. That means that our task is to believe God, stepping out in faith, trusting Him to guide us. Surrender the point in principle, and go. God doesn't steer parked cars.

So let the stones cry out.

56

DIFFERENT PRESSURES

A dedicated space for worship has a shaping and disciplinary effect. When we meet in an informal setting, as we have been doing for years, we have had to make a point of selecting music that helps us swim upstream. Because the informal surroundings make it easier for the worship to become breezy and casual, we have deliberately leaned against that. This is because the Bible tells us bluntly that our worship should be offered up with reverence and godly fear (Heb. 12:28). God is a consuming fire.

But when we have a sanctuary, and find ourselves meeting in a space bounded by classic church architecture, we are going to have to make a different set of adjustments. Hopefully, there will be no adjustments in our *theology* of worship, music, and liturgy, but we will notice—if we are paying the right kind of attention—that the natural pressures will at that time be coming from another direction.

The outside Christian culture, and our rented space, push us toward greater informality. But Christian worship ought to be familial and reverent, which is quite a different thing than the very common "come as you are" approach, the come to church in your jammies approach. We were taught to pray to *our Father*, but we were also taught to *hallow* His name. The triune God really ought to be worshiped with more than one or two chords.

But we need to start getting spiritually ready for other pressures. For example, there have been churches where the organist thinks that God will be most honored if he, the organist, shows up with pink slippers with tassels on them. There is a toney, nose-in-the-air, tall steeple, moneyed attitude that is, as far as the Holy Spirit is concerned, just another thing that the cat drug in.

Wherever you are, that is where you temptations are. Wherever you are going to be, that is where your temptations are going to be. It is very hard to anticipate the next when you are actively dealing with the other, but that is what times of transition are all about.

So let the stones cry out.

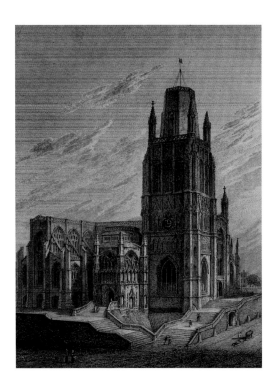

57

ELEGANT SIMPLICITY

When making our aesthetic decisions about our church building, we have to remember that simplicity is an aesthetic value. We have to remember that less is more. Some want to say that if one's good, then two's better, and that more is more.

Balance is always difficult. Some have adopted simplicity as a *moral* value, and have wound up insisting on more of it than the Bible insists on, and for the wrong reason. But nevertheless simplicity remains an aesthetic value, which is why an odd religious group like the Shakers could wind up producing beautiful furniture. They went there for the wrong reason, but they got there—at least with the rocking chairs. Others have adopted difficulty as a moral value, and they have produced some very impressive (and overdone) results.

We want our worship of God to be reverent, joyful, balanced, harmonious, scriptural... and *simple*. But when you set yourself to such a goal, you soon discover that it's complicated. Keeping it simple takes discipline and work.

We have known from the time of Aristotle that "spectacle" is an aesthetic temptation. Decadent cultures are sensate cultures, and they want distractions. They want to be impressed with things like the halftime at the Super Bowl—which for a thoughtful person resembles something from Dante's third circle.

We want a sanctuary where the Word resides, and where the people of the Word gather to hear it. We want a sanctuary where the sacraments are administered, and where the people named and shaped by the sacraments gather to partake of them. Having done so, we turn to face each other in fellowship and then we head out into another week, seeking to replicate what we have done here in the course of our lives there.

We worship, so we go out to serve. We love, so we go out to love. We sing, so we go out singing.

As we build the sanctuary we want one that houses not only what we are doing, but one that houses what we ought to be doing. And what we ought to be doing is worshiping God in gladness and simplicity of heart.

So let the stones cry out.

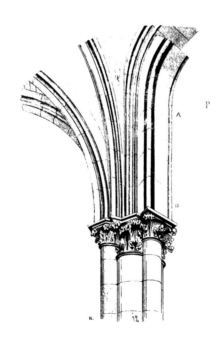

58

BARNACLES

We have noted that simplicity is an aesthetic value, and should not be regarded simply as a theological value. Too many times believers assume that if one's good, then two's better, and over the centuries the worship of God gets progressively encrusted with the barnacles of devotion.

But it is not enough simply to develop an aesthetic sense in the abstract and then go build a building that is like that. This is because the sanctuary itself, once built, will have a didactic role. Once we have a church building, and we have a generation of children who grew up worshiping God in that building, we will discover that their aesthetic sense has been trained by their surroundings. I think it was Churchill who said that first we shape our buildings, and then our buildings shape us.

The reason this is sometimes obscured is because of other factors. If you have an elegantly simple church structure, but the children growing up in it are surrounded by doctrinal and moral hypocrisies, those of them that still retain any genuine faith are going to want to get away from "all of that" as fast as they possibly can. Suppose the building is just right, but their father is given over to outbursts of anger. Suppose the building is just what it ought to be, but there is a financial scandal with the church leadership. Suppose the architect wins an award for the design, but the next generation grows up with snooty music instead of robust congregational music. In such cases, what happened is that a beautiful edifice was built in order that we might have something to chase genuine Christians away from. Call it an edifice complex.

If we are to worship the Lord in the beauty of holiness, as we are summoned by Scripture to do, then it is true that we must strive for the beauty. But at the same time, we must never neglect the holiness, and holiness is as much a reality on Tuesday as it is on the Lord's Day.

So let the stones cry out.

59

DOWN PAYMENT

When real ministry is occurring, one of the things you can expect to see is something of a mess. "Where no oxen are, the crib is clean: But much increase is by the strength of the ox" (Prov. 14:4). Dying churches are usually clean and tidy. Growing churches, flourishing churches, are characterized by "situations" that crop up, quite regularly.

In the book of Acts, the church enjoyed a rapid explosion of growth. The result of this growth was a ball drop in their mercy ministries. The Hellenistic widows were overlooked in the distribution of food (Acts 6:1). When the problem was voiced, the church addressed it forthrightly, carefully, and scripturally, appointing seven godly men to oversee the distribution. What was the result of this godly response? Well, the result was more growth (Acts 6:7).

In other words, if you address the problems caused by growth scripturally, the solution is going to be more problems caused by growth.

Building a sanctuary can be seen in two ways. One way is to see it as carving out a niche, a place where we can go to stop growing, a place where we can nurse along our market share. The sanctuary is seen as a retreat center. The other way of seeing it is to view it as a staging area, preparing for the next great advance. The former is death, the latter is what we want to insist upon.

In other words, if we are thinking that all we need to do is establish a couple of Reformed churches in Moscow, and then we can call it good, we have stepped away from the Great Commission. The house is all the elect whom God will call on the Palouse. Our sanctuary is just one part of the down payment.

So let the stones cry out.

60

ADORNED CLEAN THROUGH

The Bible teaches that the woman is the glory of the man. This is why she takes what the man provides and glorifies it. She is a glory, and she is a glorifier. The man brings home a paycheck, and she turns it into a living room, or bacon and eggs in the morning. Adornment is not a mere add-on extra; adornment is what the universe is driving toward. The woman therefore is the crown of her husband (Prov. 12:4).

But what about the Church? If this is true of wives generally, is it also true of the bride of Christ? It *is* true. The Church is described as the fullness of Him who fills everything in every way (Eph. 1:23). Christ fills the cosmos, and the Church fills Christ. Yes—just as women are called to adorn themselves, and not just externally, so also Christians are called to adorn the doctrine of the gospel (Tit. 2:10).

The Church is a woman, and is called to adornment. But she is called to adorn herself the same way individual Christian women are called to adorn themselves—with a gentle and quiet spirit *first*. God always works with both the outside and the inside, which makes sense because they are always part of the same reality. But when God cleans the *whole* cup, He does it by cleaning the inside of it first. The insides have priority.

The great harlot in Revelation is adorned. She wore purple and scarlet, and was arrayed in gold, jewels, and pearls, and had a cup full of abominations in her hand (Rev. 17:4). Her counterpart, the Christian Church, was also adorned. She was dressed in fine linen (Rev. 19:8), bright and pure. She was so great a glorious angel showed her off. She bore the glory of God, the radiance of a very rare jewel (Rev. 21:11).

So what are our plans? We hope to be able to move soon with the externals, but we are moving now on the internals. Gentle and quiet spirit, love one another, show hospitality, give yourselves away to your neighbors in the name of Jesus Christ.

So let the stones cry out.

61

THE MASTER'S FINGERS

The preacher in Ecclesiastes tells us that there is a time for everything. There is a time for birth and a time for dying. There is a time to mourn and a time to dance, and so on. Of interest to us here is that there is a time for tearing down and a time for building.

When "the time" for something arrives, there is nothing whatever that can prevent it from occurring. This means that when it is time for building, all the apparent obstacles will be manifested as just that—apparent. They will look formidable when they first present themselves, but when approached by men and women of faith they will give way in a most natural fashion. Why? Because it is time to build.

If it is not time, the most trivial things can prevent it from happening. When it is time, the most monumental obstacles will be overcome and it will seem to be the most natural thing in the world.

So the challenge is to read the times correctly. What separates presumption and faith? It is the ability to read the storyline correctly. What separates the fool from the wise man? It is knowledge of *timing*.

We are longing for God to lead us into our "time to build." We don't want to long for it so much that we run ahead, which would mean that we would run headlong. We don't want to be apathetic, such that we lag behind God's clear leading. In the wilderness, the children of Israel moved when the pillar moved—a pillar of cloud by day and fire by night—and we want to do the same thing in principle.

Some might say that it was easy for them—you can see a pillar of fire with your eyes. But the divide between the willing and the unwilling was very much obvious in the wilderness, and it is obvious now. Our task is to cultivate the demeanor found in Psalm 123:2. We want to be like the servant who has his gaze fixed on his master's fingers, eagerly waiting for direction.

So let the stones cry out.

62

LIVING STONES

When Peter describes the church, he describes us as living stones, built up into a spiritual house (1 Pet. 2:5). This house is a holy priesthood, set apart to offer up spiritual sacrifices, sacrifices that are made acceptable to God through the ultimate sacrifice of Jesus Christ. He goes on to say that there is a basic distinction between people, between those who are living stones, built up upon the cornerstone of Jesus Christ, and those who treat the cornerstone as a stone of stumbling and rock of offense.

So Jesus is either the living rock upon which all other living rock derives its life, or Jesus is the rock of catastrophe for those who were appointed to their epic disobedience. When they stumble, the text says that they stumble at the Word. This Word is what we build upon, and this Word is what they stumble over. It is the same Word, with two different responses entirely.

Now everything we do as a Christian church should be done in such a way as to testify to this glorious truth, and that should certainly include any building that we might build. The sanctuary should be an embodied Word, and this means that God's people, living stones, living sacrifices, should be attracted to it so that they might offer up the sacrifices of praise. And if no one stumbles over it then that means it is not the Word.

Whenever God's presence is made manifest in any way, what happens is that men are divided. Jesus came to bring a sword, a principle of division. In a world careening into damnation, messengers of the way of life cannot set up signposts showing the way out without controversy. Reformation and revival will not happen to the background noise of polite golf applause.

So let the stones cry out.

63

A MIND TOGETHER

We all know that character, and moods, and particular virtues and vices are characteristic of individuals. But they are also characteristic of groups of people—generations, tribes, nations, churches. You know what it is like to travel around our nation, finding that one part of the country is particularly friendly, while another is particularly industrious, and so on. People collectively have a personality. Different generations can have different personalities.

There is therefore a possibility of change from one generation to the next. There can be decline or there can be improvement—if there is change. One generation might just duplicate what went before.

Our desire should be to stay the course, remaining faithful where our fathers were faithful (2 Tim. 2:2). When our fathers were not faithful, it is our responsibility to turn away from their example, refusing to follow them in it (Ps. 78:8). In other cases, we are to build on the preparatory work done by those who went before. While David was not permitted by God to build the Temple, he had all the materials assembled so that his son would be able to (1 Chron. 22:7).

When everyone is pulling together, doing the same thing at the same time, a lot of remarkable things can happen. When Nehemiah was engaged in rebuilding the wall of Jerusalem, he had a much easier time of it when everyone was in the same mood, of the same mind. "So built we the wall; and all the wall was joined together unto the half thereof: for the people had a mind to work." (Neh. 4:6).

The people had a mind to work. This was glorious because it was the time for work. Prior to that the people had a mind to prepare, and before that, a mind to wait. The thing to pray for in all of it is a mind together.

So let the stones cry out.

love

Doughnuts

Discover deliciously divine doughnut recipes

LOVE FOOD™

First published in 2013
LOVE FOOD is an imprint of Parragon Books Ltd

Parragon
Chartist House
15-17 Trim Street
Bath, BA1 1HA

ISBN: 978-1-4723-0204-5

Printed in China

Photography by Mike Cooper
Home economy by Sumi Glass
New recipes and introduction by Angela Drake
Edited by Fiona Biggs

Notes for the Reader
This book uses both metric and imperial measurements. Follow the same units of measurement throughout; do not mix metric and imperial. All spoon measurements are level: teaspoons are assumed to be 5 ml, and tablespoons are assumed to be 15 ml. Unless otherwise stated, milk is assumed to be full fat, eggs and individual vegetables are medium, and pepper is freshly ground black pepper. Unless otherwise stated, all root vegetables should be washed in plain water and peeled prior to using.

Garnishes, decorations and serving suggestions are all optional and not necessarily included in the recipe ingredients or method. The times given are an approximate guide only. Preparation times differ according to the techniques used by different people and the cooking times may also vary from those given. Optional ingredients, variations or serving suggestions have not been included in the time calculations.

Recipes using raw or very lightly cooked eggs should be avoided by infants, the elderly, pregnant women, convalescents and anyone suffering from an illness. Pregnant and breastfeeding women are advised to avoid eating peanuts and peanut products. Sufferers from nut allergies should be aware that some of the ready-made ingredients used in the recipes in this book may contain nuts. Always check the packaging before use. Vegetarians should be aware that some of the ready-made ingredients used in the recipes in this book may contain animal products. Always check the packaging before use.

Contents

Divine Doughnuts

Smothered in a delicious sticky sweet glaze, dipped in chocolate, filled with cream, custard or jam or simply warm and dusted with sugar. Freshly made doughnuts are the ultimate sweet treat - probably not a daily one but certainly an extra-special one. This book is full of all you need to know about doughnuts, with 32 recipes from around the world including all the classics as well as baked doughnuts, cake doughnuts and savoury ones too!
So why not indulge family and friends and have a go at one or more of these fabulous doughnut recipes? You'll be surprised at just how easy they are to make!

TYPES OF DOUGHNUTS

YEAST – these are the most popular types of doughnuts. They are made with soft bread dough, usually lightly sweetened with sugar. The dough is kneaded until smooth and left in a warm place to rise before shaping and frying to get that wonderful light and open texture. This type of dough is nearly always fried.

CAKE – a quick and easy cake mixture is used to make these doughnuts. There's no need to knead the dough or leave it to rise, simply roll it out, shape it and fry. This type of mixture will result in a doughnut with a closer texture than a yeasted doughnut and a crispier crust.

BAKED CAKE – a light cake batter is used for this type of doughnut. To get the perfect ring doughnut shape you will need to invest in a doughnut tray (see essential equipment). These doughnuts have a much lighter sponge cake texture but they are quick to make, will keep for 2–3 days and are less calorific than fried doughnuts.

CHURROS – made with choux pastry dough which is usually either piped or dropped into hot oil for frying. This type of doughnut has a much lighter and more open texture than yeast or cake doughnuts. They take just minutes to make and cook – perfect when you want that fried doughnut fix.

ESSENTIAL EQUIPMENT

DOUGHNUT/COOKIE CUTTERS – if you plan to make lots of ring doughnuts it's worth buying a doughnut cutter. This handy gadget stamps the doughnut shape in one swift action. But it's almost as easy to use two round cookie cutters – one about 8 cm/3¼ inches diameter and one measuring about 2.5 cm/1 inch to cut out the holes.

LARGE DEEP PAN OR DEEP-FRYER – a deep-fryer with a built-in temperature gauge makes frying doughnuts really easy, however there's no need to rush out and buy one. A good-sized, heavy-based deep pan that can be filled to an 8-cm/3¼-inch depth with oil is perfectly suitable and easier to clean.

STAND MIXER – a stand mixer helps to make light work out of doughnut-making. They come with a paddle attachment for mixing and a dough hook for kneading.

THERMOMETER – a sugar thermometer will ensure that you heat the oil to the correct temperature for frying. It needs to be made of brass or metal and measure up to a temperature of at least 200°C/400°F.

DOUGHNUT PANS – for baked cake doughnuts you'll need a doughnut tray that has 6 or 12 moulded doughnut ring-shaped dips. The mixture is then piped or spooned into the dips before baking in the oven. You can also buy mini doughnut pans – ideal for bite-sized sweet treats.

PIPING BAG AND NOZZLES – for piping churros into hot oil or filling doughnut trays with batter a large piping bag is useful. Buy a reusable plastic bag or a roll of sturdy disposable bags. A few different sized plain and fluted nozzles are handy too.

ESSENTIAL INGREDIENTS

You only need a few ingredients for most of the recipes in this book. Here's a guide to some of the basics...

EASY-BLEND DRIED YEAST – unlike fresh or ordinary dried yeast that has to be activated in warm sweetened liquid before adding to the dry ingredients, easy-blend (or fast action) yeast is just stirred into the flour. If you use ordinary dried yeast then mix it with some of the warm liquid and sugar or honey from the recipe and leave for 15 minutes until frothy before adding it to the flour with the rest of the liquid.

FLOUR – for yeast-based doughnuts it's vital to use a strong plain flour with a high gluten content. This allows the dough to be kneaded and stretched and will result in a light and airy textured doughnut. For cake and baked doughnuts use either plain or self-raising flour with baking powder or bicarbonate of soda as the raising agent.

SUGAR – caster sugar which has a fine texture that dissolves easily is best for sweetening the doughnut mixture, but caster, granulated or icing sugar can be used to coat the warm cooked doughnuts.

OIL – choose a light flavourless oil that can be heated to a high temperature for frying the doughnuts. Sunflower, peanut or good quality vegetable oil are all fine. You can use the same oil for two–three batches of frying but always strain after each use and discard the oil when it starts to turn a darker colour.

EGGS – eggs enrich yeast dough and are essential for a cake or baked dough. Allow to come to room temperature before using.

TIPS FOR MAKING YEAST DOUGH

- Don't overheat the liquid – it should be quite warm but not too hot or it will kill the yeast and the dough won't rise.
- It's better to have a soft, sticky dough and gradually incorporate more flour than a dry and crumbly dough which will be hard to knead and take longer to rise.
- Once the doughnuts have been shaped, don't leave them for too long before frying as they can over-prove and lose their shape.

TIPS FOR FRYING DOUGHNUTS

- If you are using a pan of oil don't over-fill it – there should be at least 5 cm/2 inches from the top of the oil to the rim of the pan.
- It's essential to maintain the correct temperature when frying the doughnuts. If the temperature is too high they will overbrown but not cook through. If it's too low the doughnuts will take longer to cook and absorb more oil making them soggy and fatty.
- Don't overcrowd the fryer or pan with doughnuts as this will reduce the temperature of the oil.
- Never leave hot oil unattended as it can be dangerous.

TIPS FOR BAKING DOUGHNUTS

- Thoroughly grease the doughnut pan before use with either softened or melted butter or a cooking spray.
- Don't overfill the rings or you'll lose the doughnut shape during baking. Piping the mixture is the best way to evenly fill the tray, but if the mixture has fruit in it then carefully spoon it in with a teaspoon, wiping away any spills with kitchen paper.
- Take care not to over-cook baked doughnuts or they will have a dry texture. The doughnuts should just spring back when lightly pressed with your fingertips.

Simple Doughnuts

MAKES | PREP | COOK
12 | **45** | **25** MINUTES

PLUS RISING & CHILLING

INGREDIENTS

225 ml/8 fl oz milk

3 tbsp easy-blend
dried yeast

250 g/9 oz plain flour,
plus extra for dusting

2 tbsp caster sugar

½ tsp salt

3 egg yolks

1 tsp vanilla extract

55 g/2 oz butter, softened

oil, for greasing
and frying

GLAZE (OPTIONAL)

200 g/7 oz icing sugar

3–4 tbsp water or
full-fat milk

1. Heat the milk until lukewarm and dissolve the yeast into the milk. Add 200 g/7 oz of the flour into the mixture and set aside for 30 minutes.

2. Using a stand mixer fitted with a paddle attachment, add the sugar, salt, egg yolks and vanilla to the bowl and mix on a low speed until smooth. Add the butter and milk and mix slowly.

3. Change the paddle attachment to a dough hook and add the remaining flour. Mix slowly until the dough is smooth. Refrigerate the mixture for 1 hour.

4. Lightly grease a baking tray. Roll the dough on a floured surface. The dough should be about 1 cm/½ inch thick. Use a doughnut cutter to cut out the doughnuts.

5. Place on the greased baking tray, cover with clingfilm and leave in a warm place. The doughnuts should rise to nearly double the original size and spring back when touched.

6. Heat enough oil for deep-frying in a large saucepan or deep-fryer to 180-190°C/350-375°F, or until a cube of bread browns in 30 seconds. Carefully place the doughnuts, one at a time, into the hot oil. Fry for 2 minutes or until golden brown. Remove with a slotted spoon and drain on kitchen paper.

7. To make the glaze, place the sugar in a bowl and slowly mix in the water or milk until smooth. Pour over the cooled doughnuts.

Simple yet delicious, these classic doughnuts are the perfect treat, with or without the icing sugar glaze.

Jam Doughnuts

MAKES **10**   PREP **25**   COOK **25** MINUTES

PLUS RISING

INGREDIENTS

oil, for greasing
and frying

450 g/1 lb strong
white flour, plus extra
for dusting

55 g/2 oz butter,
cut into pieces

2 tbsp caster sugar

½ tsp salt

2¼ tsp easy-blend dried
yeast

1 egg, lightly beaten

175 ml/6 fl oz lukewarm
milk

FILLING

150 g/5½ oz seedless
strawberry or raspberry jam

---

1. Lightly grease a large bowl and 2 baking trays.

2. Place the flour in a large bowl, add the butter and rub it in until the mixture resembles breadcrumbs. Stir in the sugar, salt and yeast. Make a well in the centre and add the egg and milk, then mix to form a soft, pliable dough. Knead well for 10 minutes.

3. Place in the greased bowl and cover. Leave in a warm place to rise for about 1 hour or until doubled in size.

4. Knead the dough on a floured work surface, then divide into 10 pieces. Shape each piece into a ball and place on the prepared baking trays. Cover and leave in a warm place to double in size for 45 minutes.

5. Heat enough oil for deep-frying in a large saucepan or deep-fryer to 180-190°C/350-375°F, or until a cube of bread browns in 30 seconds. Deep-fry the doughnuts in batches for 2-3 minutes each side. Remove with a slotted spoon, drain on kitchen paper and dust with sugar.

6. To fill the doughnuts, spoon the jam into a piping bag fitted with a plain nozzle. Insert a sharp knife into each doughnut and twist to make a hole. Push the point of the nozzle into the hole and pipe in some jam.

Why not try blueberry or apricot jam — or any other type of jam you like — for a different taste experience.

Baked Ring
Doughnuts

MAKES	PREP	COOK
16	**20**	**45** MINUTES

INGREDIENTS

225 g/8 oz self-raising flour

1½ tsp baking powder

175 g/6 oz caster sugar

½ tsp salt

150 ml/5 fl oz milk

2 eggs, beaten

½ tsp vanilla extract

40 g/1½ oz butter, melted, plus extra for greasing

SUGAR COATING

4 tbsp caster sugar

2–3 tsp ground cinnamon

1. Preheat the oven to 190°C/375°F/Gas Mark 5. Grease a 6-hole doughnut tin.

2. Sift together the flour and baking powder into a bowl and stir in the sugar and salt. Make a well in the centre. Mix together the milk, eggs, vanilla extract and butter and pour into the well. Mix until smooth.

3. Spoon the mixture into a large piping bag fitted with a plain nozzle. Pipe some of the mixture into the prepared tin, filling each hole about two-thirds full. Bake in the preheated oven for 10–15 minutes, or until risen, golden and just firm to the touch. Leave to cool in the tin for 5 minutes, then turn out onto a wire rack. Bake the remaining mixture in the same way, rinsing and greasing the pan each time, to make 16 doughnuts in total.

4. To make the sugar coating, mix together the sugar and cinnamon on a plate. Gently toss each warm doughnut in the cinnamon sugar to coat completely. Serve warm or cold.

Made with a simple cake batter instead of yeast dough these baked doughnuts have a lovely light texture and will keep fresh for longer than deep-fried doughnuts.

Custard Doughnuts

MAKES **8** PREP **45** COOK **20** MINUTES
PLUS RISING

INGREDIENTS

175 ml/6 fl oz milk

25 g/1 oz butter

350 g/12 oz strong white flour, plus extra for dusting and kneading

½ tsp salt

1½ tsp easy-blend dried yeast

25 g/1 oz caster sugar, plus extra for coating

1 egg, beaten

oil, for deep-frying and greasing

4 tbsp seedless raspberry jam

FILLING

2 eggs

55 g/2 oz caster sugar

1 tsp vanilla extract

3 tbsp cornflour

450 ml/16 fl oz milk

1. Put the milk and butter into a small saucepan over a low heat and heat until the butter has melted. Leave to cool for 5 minutes.

2. Sift the flour into a large bowl and stir in the salt, yeast and sugar. Pour in the milk mixture and the egg and mix to a soft dough. Turn out the dough onto a floured surface and knead for 5–6 minutes, until smooth and elastic, adding a little more flour if needed.

3. Put the dough into a bowl, cover and leave to stand in a warm place for 1 hour, or until doubled in size. Line two large baking sheets with baking paper.

4. Knock back the dough and divide into 8 pieces. Shape each piece into a 13-cm/5-inch length. Place on the prepared baking sheets and cover with lightly oiled clingfilm. Leave to stand in a warm place for 10–15 minutes, until puffy.

5. Heat enough oil for deep-frying in a large saucepan or deep-fryer to 180–190°C/350–375°F, or until a cube of bread browns in 30 seconds. Add the doughnuts, 2–3 at a time, and fry on each side for 1–2 minutes, or until golden. Remove and drain on kitchen paper, then toss in sugar to coat. Leave to cool.

6. To make the filling, put the eggs, sugar, vanilla extract and cornflour into a bowl and whisk together until smooth. Put the milk into a saucepan over a medium heat and heat until almost boiling, then whisk it into the egg mixture. Return the custard to the pan and cook, whisking constantly, for 8–10 minutes, until smooth and thickened. Transfer to a bowl, cover the surface with greaseproof paper and leave to cool completely.

7. Split the doughnuts lengthways and spread jam down the centre of each one. Spoon the custard into a large piping bag fitted with a star-shaped nozzle and pipe the custard on top of the jam.

Split and filled with jam and a vanilla pastry cream, these doughnuts make the perfect tea-time treat. Replace the pastry cream with whipped cream, if you prefer.

Yum Yums

MAKES **16** PREP **40** COOK **15** MINUTES

PLUS RISING

INGREDIENTS

175 ml/6 fl oz milk

25 g/1 oz butter

350 g/12 oz strong white flour, plus extra for dusting and kneading

½ tsp salt

1½ tsp easy-blend dried yeast

40 g/1½ oz caster sugar

2 tsp finely grated lemon rind

1 egg, beaten

oil, for deep-frying and greasing

GLAZE

175 g/6 oz icing sugar

4 tbsp lemon juice

1. Put the milk and butter into a small saucepan over a low heat and heat until the butter has melted. Leave to cool for 5 minutes.

2. Sift the flour into a large bowl and stir in the salt, yeast, sugar and lemon rind. Pour in the milk mixture and the egg and mix to a soft dough. Turn out the dough onto a floured surface and knead for 5–6 minutes, until smooth and elastic, adding a little more flour if needed. Put the dough into a bowl, cover and leave in a warm place for 1 hour, or until doubled in size. Line two large baking sheets with baking paper.

3. Knock back the dough and roll out to a 25 x 31 cm/10 x 12½ inch rectangle. Cut the dough into 16 short strips and tightly twist each strip 2–3 times. Place the doughnuts on the prepared baking sheets and cover with lightly oiled clingfilm. Leave to stand in a warm place for 10 minutes, until puffy.

4. Heat enough oil for deep-frying in a large saucepan or deep-fryer to 180–190°C/350–375°F, or until a cube of bread browns in 30 seconds. Add the doughnuts, 2–3 at a time, and fry on each side for 1–2 minutes, or until golden. Remove with a slotted spoon and drain on kitchen paper.

5. To make the glaze, mix together the icing sugar and lemon juice until smooth. When the doughnuts are just cool enough to handle, dip each one in the lemon glaze to coat. Leave to set on a wire rack.

These short twists of dough with a lemon glaze are simple to make. Don't worry if they un-twist a little when fried — they will still taste delicious!

Coconut Doughnuts

MAKES **12** PREP **20** COOK **30** MINUTES

INGREDIENTS

175 g/6 oz self-raising flour

1 tsp baking powder

115 g/4 oz caster sugar

¼ tsp salt

150 ml/5 fl oz coconut milk

1 egg, lightly beaten

25 g/1 oz butter, melted, plus extra for greasing

100 g/3½ oz desiccated coconut

5 tbsp seedless raspberry jam, warmed

1. Preheat the oven to 190°C/375°F/Gas Mark 5. Grease a 6-hole doughnut tin.

2. Sift together the flour and baking powder into a bowl and stir in the sugar and salt. Make a well in the centre. Mix together the coconut milk, egg and butter, pour into the well and mix until smooth. Stir in 25 g/1 oz of the coconut.

3. Spoon the mixture into a large piping bag fitted with a plain nozzle. Pipe half the mixture into the doughnut holes. Bake in the preheated oven for 10–15 minutes, until risen, golden and just firm to the touch. Leave to cool in the tin for 5 minutes, then turn out onto a wire rack. Rinse and regrease the doughnut tin and repeat with the remaining mixture to make 12 doughnuts in total.

4. Sprinkle the remaining coconut over a large flat plate. Brush the warm doughnuts all over with the warm jam and dip in the coconut to coat completely. Serve warm or cold.

These light-as-air baked doughnuts are brushed with warm jam, then smothered in desiccated coconut. To give them a nuttier flavour, lightly toast the coconut.

Apple Doughnuts

MAKES **PREP** **COOK**
16 **40** **20** MINUTES
PLUS RISING

INGREDIENTS

275 ml/9½ fl oz milk
40 g/1½ oz butter
500 g/1 lb 2 oz strong white flour, plus extra for dusting and kneading
½ tsp salt
2 tsp easy-blend dried yeast
55 g/2 oz caster sugar
2 tsp ground cinnamon
1 large egg, beaten
1 large eating apple, peeled, cored and diced
oil, for deep-frying and greasing

GLAZE

140 g/5 oz icing sugar
1 tsp ground cinnamon
2 tbsp milk

1. Put the milk and butter into a small saucepan over a low heat and heat until the butter has melted. Leave to cool for 5 minutes.

2. Sift the flour into a large bowl and stir in the salt, yeast, sugar and cinnamon. Pour in the milk mixture and egg and mix to a soft dough. Turn out onto a floured surface and knead for 5–6 minutes, until smooth and elastic, adding a little more flour if needed. Flatten the dough, spoon over the diced apple and knead into the dough for 2 minutes.

3. Place the dough in a bowl, cover and leave in a warm place for 1 hour, or until doubled in size. Line two large baking sheets with baking paper.

4. Knock back the dough and roll out on a floured surface to a thickness of 15 mm/⅝ inch. Use an 8-cm/3¼-inch round cutter to stamp out 12 doughnuts. Lightly re-knead the trimmings, roll out and stamp out another 4 doughnuts. Place the doughnuts on the prepared baking sheets and cover with lightly oiled clingfilm. Leave in a warm place for 10 minutes, until puffy.

5. Heat enough oil for deep-frying in a large saucepan or deep-fryer to 180–190°C/350–375°F, or until a cube of bread browns in 30 seconds. Add the doughnuts, a few at a time, and fry on each side for 1–2 minutes, or until golden. Remove with a slotted spoon and drain on kitchen paper.

6. To make the glaze, put the icing sugar, cinnamon and milk into a bowl and mix together until smooth. When the doughnuts are just cool enough to handle, dip the top of each in the glaze. Transfer to a wire rack to set.

Chunks of sweet apple and ground cinnamon give these deep-fried doughnuts a wonderful spiced fruit flavour. They are best eaten warm, just after the glaze has set.

Beignets

INGREDIENTS

100 ml/3½ fl oz lukewarm water

2 tsp easy-blend dried yeast

55 g/2 oz caster sugar

½ tsp salt

1 egg, beaten

175 ml/6 fl oz evaporated milk, warmed

450 g/1 lb strong white flour, plus extra for dusting and kneading

25 g/1 oz white vegetable fat, softened

oil, for deep-frying

55 g/2 oz icing sugar

1. Put the water into a large bowl and whisk in the yeast. Add the sugar, salt, egg and evaporated milk and whisk to combine. Stir in half the flour and mix to a smooth batter. Beat in the vegetable fat. Add the remaining flour and mix to a soft dough.

2. Turn out the dough onto a lightly floured surface and knead for 4–5 minutes, until smooth and elastic, adding a little more flour if needed. Put the dough into a bowl, cover and leave in a warm place for about 2 hours, or until doubled in size.

3. Heat enough oil for deep-frying in a large saucepan or deep-fryer to 180–190°C/350–375°F, or until a cube of bread browns in 30 seconds.

4. Meanwhile, knock back the dough and roll out on a lightly floured surface to a thickness of 8 mm/³⁄₈ inch. Use a sharp knife to cut the dough into about 30 squares.

5. Add the squares, about 4 at a time, to the hot oil and fry on each side for 1–2 minutes, or until puffed up and deep golden brown. Baste the top of the beignets during frying by gently spooning hot oil over them – this will help them to puff up. Remove with a slotted spoon and drain on kitchen paper. Thickly dust with icing sugar and serve immediately.

These puffed up, pillow-shaped doughnuts generously dusted with icing sugar are popular in cafés in the French quarter of New Orleans.

Chocolate Cake
Doughnuts

MAKES **14**   PREP **25**   COOK **55** MINUTES

PLUS RESTING

INGREDIENTS

125 ml/4 fl oz milk, warmed
1 egg
1 tsp vanilla extract
30 g/1 oz cocoa powder
225 g/8 oz plain flour
½ tsp bicarbonate of soda
½ tsp baking powder
½ tsp salt
100 g/3½ oz caster sugar
25 g/1 oz butter
oil, for frying

GLAZE

40 g/1½ oz plain chocolate, broken into pieces
40 g/1½ oz white chocolate, broken into pieces

1. Blend together the warmed milk, egg and vanilla extract in a bowl.

2. Using a stand mixer with a paddle attachment, mix the cocoa powder, flour, bicarbonate of soda, baking powder, salt and sugar together. Add the butter and blend. Slowly add the milk, egg and vanilla. Mix until the batter is smooth and thick and resembles a biscuit dough.

3. Leave the dough to rest in the mixer for 20 minutes.

4. Roll the dough out on a floured surface. The dough should be 1 cm/ ½ inch thick. Using a doughnut cutter, stamp out 14 doughnuts.

5. Heat enough oil for deep-frying in a large saucepan or deep-fryer to 180-190°C/350-375°F, or until a cube of bread browns in 30 seconds. Carefully place the doughnuts, one at a time, into the oil. Fry for 2 minutes on each side, or until golden brown. Remove with a slotted spoon and drain on kitchen paper.

6. To make the glaze, melt each of the chocolates separately in heatproof bowls set over pans of simmering water. Coat the doughnuts, drizzling the chocolates in a pattern.

You'll find it hard to stop at just one after trying these utterly delectable doughnuts...

S'mores Doughnuts

MAKES **12** PREP **45** COOK **16** MINUTES

PLUS RISING

INGREDIENTS

150 ml/5 fl oz milk

25 g/1 oz white vegetable fat

300 g/10½ oz strong white flour, plus extra for dusting and kneading

¼ tsp salt

1½ tsp easy-blend dried yeast

2 tbsp caster sugar, plus extra for coating

1 large egg, beaten

12 small squares plain chocolate

48 mini white marshmallows

oil, for deep frying and greasing

1 small digestive biscuit, crushed

GLAZE

55 g/2 oz icing sugar, sifted

2 tbsp water

1. Put the milk and vegetable fat into a small saucepan over a low heat and heat until the fat has melted. Leave to cool for 5 minutes.

2. Sift the flour into a large bowl and stir in the salt, yeast and sugar. Pour in the milk mixture and the egg and mix to a soft dough. Turn out the dough onto a floured surface and knead for 5–6 minutes, until smooth and elastic, adding a little more flour if needed.

3. Place the dough in a bowl, cover and leave in a warm place for 1 hour, or until doubled in size. Line a large baking sheet with baking paper.

4. Knock back the dough and divide into 12 pieces. Roll out each piece to a 9-cm/3½-inch round and place a square of chocolate and 4 mini marshmallows in the centre. Gather up the dough to enclose the filling, tightly pinching the edges together to seal. Place on the prepared baking sheet join side down and flatten each doughnut slightly with the palm of your hand. Cover with lightly oiled clingfilm and leave to stand in a warm place for 8–10 minutes, until puffy.

5. Heat enough oil for deep-frying in a large saucepan or deep-fryer to 180–190°C/350–375°F, or until a cube of bread browns in 30 seconds. Fry the doughnuts, 3 at a time, for 1–2 minutes on each side or until golden. Remove and drain on kitchen paper.

6. To make the glaze, put the icing sugar and water into a bowl and beat together until smooth. Dip the top of each warm doughnut in the glaze and sprinkle over the biscuit crumbs. Serve warm.

The only way to eat these delicious doughnuts is while they are warm and the hidden middle of chocolate and marshmallow is still molten.

Honey & Pistachio Mini Doughnuts

MAKES	PREP	COOK
24	**20**	**20** MINUTES

INGREDIENTS

115 g/4 oz self-raising flour

½ tsp baking powder

pinch of salt

55 g/2 oz butter, softened, plus extra for greasing

55 g/2 oz caster sugar

1 egg, beaten

6 tbsp milk

40 g/1½ oz pistachio nuts, finely chopped

GLAZE

85 g/3 oz icing sugar

1 tbsp clear honey, warmed

2 tsp milk

1. Preheat the oven to 190°C/375°F/Gas Mark 5. Grease a 12-hole mini doughnut tin. Sift together the flour, baking powder and salt into a bowl.

2. Put the butter and sugar into a bowl and beat together until pale and fluffy. Gradually beat in the egg, then stir in half the flour mixture. Beat in the milk, then fold in the remaining flour mixture and three quarters of the chopped nuts.

3. Spoon the mixture into a large, disposable piping bag. Snip off the end and pipe half the filling into the doughnut holes, filling each one about two-thirds full.

4. Bake in the preheated oven for 8–10 minutes, until risen, pale golden and just firm to the touch. Leave to cool in the tin for 2–3 minutes, then transfer to a wire rack. Bake the remaining mixture in the same way, rinsing and greasing the tin before filling.

5. To make the glaze, sift the icing sugar into a bowl and stir in the warm honey and milk to make a smooth glaze. Dip the top of each doughnut into the glaze then sprinkle with the remaining chopped nuts.

These dainty little baked cake doughnuts are just perfect for serving with afternoon tea. You can replace the pistachios with walnuts or hazelnuts, if you prefer.

Lemon Churros with Orange
Dipping Sauce

MAKES **20**   PREP **20**   COOK **25** MINUTES

INGREDIENTS

100 g/3½ oz unsalted butter, diced

300 ml/10 fl oz water

140 g/5 oz plain flour, sifted

large pinch of salt

2 large eggs, beaten

finely grated rind of 1 large lemon

oil, for deep-frying

icing sugar, for dusting

ORANGE SAUCE

1 tbsp arrowroot

300 ml/10 fl oz fresh orange juice

40 g/1½ oz caster sugar

1. To make the orange sauce, blend the arrowroot to a smooth paste with 2 tablespoons of the orange juice and set aside. Put the remaining juice and the sugar into a small saucepan over a low heat and heat until the sugar has dissolved. Add the blended arrowroot and simmer gently, stirring constantly, for 4–5 minutes, until just thickened. Remove from the heat, cover and keep warm.

2. Put the butter and water into a large saucepan over a medium heat and heat until the butter has melted. Bring to the boil, remove from the heat and tip in the flour and salt. Beat thoroughly until the mixture is smooth and comes away from the side of the pan. Leave to cool for 5 minutes, then gradually beat in the eggs to make a thick and glossy paste. Beat in the lemon rind.

3. Heat enough oil for deep-frying in a large saucepan or deep-fryer to 180–190°C/350–375°F, or until a cube of bread browns in 30 seconds. Spoon the paste into a large piping bag fitted with a large star nozzle and pipe 4–5 short loops of the paste into the hot oil. Fry, turning frequently, for 2–3 minutes, until crisp and golden. Remove with a slotted spoon and drain on kitchen paper. Keep warm while frying the remaining mixture.

4. Thickly dust the hot churros with icing sugar and serve immediately with the orange sauce for dipping.

The tangy lemon flavouring ensures
that these warm Mexican-style
doughnuts are not too sweet, even with
a generous dusting of icing sugar.

Chocolate-coated Doughnut Holes

MAKES **45**   PREP **40**   COOK **20** MINUTES

PLUS RISING

INGREDIENTS

175 ml/6 fl oz milk

40 g/1½ oz butter

300 g/10½ oz strong white flour, plus extra for dusting and kneading

1 tbsp cocoa powder

2 tsp ground cinnamon

¼ tsp salt

1½ tsp easy-blend dried yeast

2 tbsp caster sugar

1 large egg, beaten

oil, for deep-frying and greasing

140 g/5 oz plain chocolate, broken into pieces

140 g/5 oz white chocolate, broken into pieces

chocolate vermicelli or hundreds and thousands, to decorate (optional)

1. Put the milk and butter into a small saucepan over a low heat and heat until the butter has melted. Leave to cool for 5 minutes.

2. Sift together the flour and cocoa powder into a large bowl and stir in the cinnamon, salt, yeast and sugar. Pour in the milk mixture and the egg and mix to a soft dough. Turn out the dough onto a floured surface and knead for 5–6 minutes, until smooth and elastic, adding a little more flour if needed.

3. Put the dough into a bowl, cover and leave in a warm place for 1 hour, or until doubled in size. Line three baking sheets with baking paper.

4. Knock back the dough and roll out on a lightly floured surface to a thickness of 15 mm/⅝ inch. Using a 2.5-cm/1-inch cookie cutter, stamp out about 45 rounds, re-rolling the dough as necessary. Place the rounds on two of the prepared baking sheets and cover with lightly oiled clingfilm. Leave to stand in a warm place for 5–10 minutes, until puffy.

5. Heat enough oil for deep-frying in a large saucepan or deep-fryer to 180–190°C/350–375°F, or until a cube of bread browns in 30 seconds. Add the rounds, 6–8 at a time, and fry for 2–3 minutes until golden, gently turning them in the hot oil all the time. Remove with a slotted spoon and drain on kitchen paper. Leave to cool.

6. Put the plain chocolate and white chocolate into two separate heatproof bowls set over saucepans of simmering water and heat until melted. Leave to cool for 5 minutes, then dip half the doughnut holes in plain chocolate to completely coat and dip the remaining holes in white chocolate. Top with chocolate vermicelli or hundreds and thousands, if using. Transfer to the remaining prepared baking sheet and leave to set.

For some the best bit of the doughnut is the hole — so why not just make a whole batch of them? These chocolate-coated ones are perfect for a children's party.

Baked Blueberry Doughnuts

MAKES **12**   PREP **20**   COOK **30** MINUTES

INGREDIENTS

200 g/7 oz self-raising flour
1 tsp baking powder
115 g/4 oz caster sugar
¼ tsp salt
125 ml/4 fl oz buttermilk
2 large eggs, beaten
½ tsp vanilla extract
25 g/1 oz butter, melted,
  plus extra for greasing
125 g/4½ oz small fresh
  blueberries

GLAZE

115 g/4 oz icing sugar
2 tbsp milk
1 tsp vanilla extract

1. Preheat the oven to 190°C/375°F/Gas Mark 5. Grease a 6-hole doughnut tin.

2. Sift together the flour and baking powder into a bowl and stir in the sugar and salt. Make a well in the centre. Put the buttermilk, eggs, vanilla extract and melted butter into a jug, mix together and pour into the well. Mix until smooth, then gently fold in the blueberries.

3. Using a teaspoon, carefully spoon half the mixture into the prepared tin, taking care not to overfill the holes – they should be about two-thirds full. Bake in the preheated oven for 12–15 minutes, or until risen, golden and just firm to the touch. Leave to cool in the tin for 5 minutes, then turn out onto a wire rack. Rinse and regrease the tin and repeat with the remaining mixture.

4. To make the glaze, sift the icing sugar into a bowl and beat in the milk and vanilla extract until smooth. Spoon the glaze over the doughnuts, letting it run down the sides. Leave to set.

Full of plump fresh blueberries, these doughnuts
have a wonderful fruity flavour, perfectly
complemented by the sweet vanilla glaze.

Cookies & Cream
Doughnuts

MAKES | PREP | COOK
12 | **45** | **20** MINUTES

PLUS RISING

INGREDIENTS

175 ml/6 fl oz milk

25 g/1 oz butter

350 g/12 oz strong white flour, plus extra for dusting and kneading

¼ tsp salt

1½ tsp easy-blend dried yeast

25 g/1 oz caster sugar, plus extra for coating

1 egg, beaten

oil, for deep-frying and greasing

4 tbsp seedless raspberry jam

FILLING

450 ml/16 fl oz double cream

70 g/2½ oz chocolate sandwich cookies

GLAZE

140 g/5 oz icing sugar

2 tbsp water

1. Put the milk and butter into a small saucepan over a low heat and heat until the butter has melted. Leave to cool for 5 minutes.

2. Sift the flour into a large bowl and stir in the salt, yeast and sugar. Pour in the milk mixture and the egg and mix to a soft dough. Turn out the dough onto a floured surface and knead for 5–6 minutes, until smooth and elastic, adding a little more flour if needed.

3. Put the dough into a bowl, cover and leave in a warm place for 1 hour, or until doubled in size. Line two large baking sheets with baking paper.

4. Knock back the dough and roll out on a lightly floured surface to a thickness of 1 cm/½ inch. Using a 9-cm/3½-inch doughnut cutter, stamp out 8 doughnuts. Lightly re-knead the trimmings, roll out and stamp out another 4 doughnuts. Place on the prepared baking sheets. Cover with lightly oiled clingfilm and leave in a warm place for 10 minutes, until puffy.

5. Heat enough oil for deep-frying in a large saucepan or deep-fryer to 180–190°C/350–375°F, or until a cube of bread browns in 30 seconds. Add the doughnuts, 2–3 at a time, and fry on each side for 1–2 minutes, or until golden. Remove and drain on kitchen paper. Leave to cool.

6. To make the filling, whip the cream until it holds soft peaks. Roughly crush the cookies and fold into the cream, reserving 2 tablespoons for decoration.

7. To make the glaze, sift the icing sugar into a bowl and beat in the water until smooth.

8. Halve each doughnut horizontally and spread the jam on the bottom halves. Spoon the filling on top of the jam. Dip each top half in the glaze and place on top of the cream filling. Sprinkle over the reserved crushed cookies and leave to set.

With a lovely sweet cream filling, these doughnuts are perfect for a special occasion. They can be made the day before and kept in the refrigerator overnight.

Rocky Road
Doughnuts

MAKES **8** PREP **40** COOK **20** MINUTES
PLUS RISING

INGREDIENTS

175 ml/6 fl oz milk

40 g/1½ oz butter

280 g/10 oz strong white flour, plus extra for dusting and kneading

2 tbsp cocoa powder

¼ tsp salt

1½ tsp easy-blend dried yeast

2 tbsp caster sugar

1 large egg, beaten

oil, for deep-frying and greasing

TOPPING

115 g/4 oz milk chocolate, broken into pieces

40 g/1½ oz unsalted butter

3 tbsp chopped mixed nuts

40 g/1½ oz mini pink and white marshmallows

25 g/1 oz glacé cherries, chopped

1. Put the milk and butter into a small saucepan over a low heat and heat until the butter has melted. Leave to cool for 5 minutes.

2. Sift together the flour and cocoa powder into a large bowl and stir in the salt, yeast and sugar. Pour in the milk mixture and the egg and mix to a soft dough. Turn out the dough onto a floured surface and knead for 5–6 minutes, until smooth and elastic, adding a little more flour if needed.

3. Put the dough into a bowl, cover and leave in a warm place for 1–1½ hours, or until doubled in size. Line a large baking sheet with baking paper.

4. Knock back the dough and roll out on a lightly floured surface to a thickness of 1½ cm/⅝ inch. Using a 9-cm/3½-inch doughnut cutter, stamp out 6 doughnuts. Lightly re-knead the trimmings, roll out and stamp out another 2 doughnuts. Place on the prepared baking sheet. Cover with lightly oiled clingfilm and leave in a warm place for 10 minutes, until puffy.

5. Heat enough oil for deep-frying in a large saucepan or deep-fryer to 180–190°C/350–375°F, or until a cube of bread browns in 30 seconds. Add the doughnuts, a few at a time, and fry on each side for 1–2 minutes, or until golden. Remove with a slotted spoon and drain on kitchen paper. Leave to cool.

6. To make the topping, put the chocolate and butter into a heatproof bowl set over a saucepan of gently simmering water and heat until melted. Stir until smooth, then leave to cool for 5 minutes. Dip each doughnut in the chocolate glaze and place on a wire rack. Top with the nuts, marshmallows and cherries and drizzle over any remaining chocolate sauce. Leave to set.

These indulgent chocolate doughnuts
have a smooth milk chocolate
glaze and are loaded with nuts,
marshmallows and cherries.

Churros

INGREDIENTS

225 ml/8 fl oz water

85 g/3 oz butter or lard, diced

2 tbsp dark muscovado sugar

finely grated rind of 1 small orange (optional)

pinch of salt

175 g/6 oz plain flour, well sifted

1 tsp ground cinnamon, plus extra for dusting

1 tsp vanilla extract

2 eggs

oil, for deep-frying

caster sugar, for dusting

1. Heat the water, butter, muscovado sugar, orange rind, if using, and salt in a heavy-based saucepan over a medium heat until the butter has melted.

2. Add the flour, all at once, the cinnamon and vanilla extract, then remove the saucepan from the heat and beat rapidly until the mixture pulls away from the side of the saucepan.

3. Leave to cool slightly, then beat in the eggs, one at a time, beating well after each addition, until the mixture is thick and smooth. Spoon into a piping bag fitted with a wide star nozzle.

4. Heat enough oil for deep-frying in a deep-fryer or deep saucepan to 180–190°C/350–375°F, or until a cube of bread browns in 30 seconds. Pipe 13-cm/5-inch lengths about 7.5 cm/3 inches apart into the hot oil. Fry for 2–3 minutes, turning frequently until crisp and golden. Remove with a slotted spoon and drain on kitchen paper. Keep warm while frying the remaining mixture.

5. Dust the churros with caster sugar and cinnamon and serve.

Served either hot from the saucepan
or cooled to room temperature,
churros make a delicious treat.

Powdered Doughnuts

MAKES **8**   PREP **35**   COOK **15** MINUTES

PLUS CHILLING

INGREDIENTS

250 g/9 oz self-raising flour,
plus extra for dusting

1½ tsp baking powder

½ tsp mixed spice

¼ tsp salt

55 g/2 oz caster sugar

1 large egg, beaten

100 ml/3½ fl oz milk

25 g/1 oz butter, melted
and slightly cooled

½ tsp vanilla extract

oil, for deep-frying

115 g/4 oz icing sugar, plus
extra if needed, for dusting

1. Sift together the flour, baking powder and mixed spice into a large bowl. Stir in the salt and sugar. Make a well in the centre.

2. Put the egg, milk, butter and vanilla extract into a jug, mix together and pour into the well. Mix to a medium–soft dough, adding a little extra flour if the dough is too sticky to handle. Cover and chill in the refrigerator for 30 minutes.

3. Roll out the dough on a lightly floured surface to a thickness of 15 mm/⅝ inch. Use a 7.5-cm/3-inch doughnut cutter to stamp out 8 doughnuts

4. Heat enough oil for deep-frying in a large saucepan or deep-fryer to 180–190°C/350–375°F, or until a cube of bread browns in 30 seconds. Add the doughnuts, 3–4 at a time, and fry, turning frequently, for 3–4 minutes, or until crisp and deep golden. Remove and drain on kitchen paper. Leave to cool for 10 minutes.

5. Sift the icing sugar into a shallow bowl and toss the doughnuts in it to coat thoroughly. Serve immediately, before the icing sugar dissolves into the warm doughnuts – if this does happen, just dust liberally with more icing sugar.

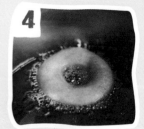

Delicious warm, crisp and golden fried doughnuts without having to wait for dough to rise — that's the beauty of these yeast-free doughnuts.

French Crullers

INGREDIENTS

55 g/2 oz butter
125 ml/4 fl oz water
2 tsp caster sugar
115 g/4 oz self-raising flour
large pinch of salt
2 eggs
1 egg white
oil, for deep-frying

GLAZE

225 g/8 oz icing sugar
4 tbsp milk

1. Put the butter, water and sugar into a large saucepan over a medium heat and heat until the butter has melted. Bring to the boil, remove from the heat and tip in the flour and salt. Beat thoroughly until the mixture is smooth and comes away from the side of the pan. Return to the heat and cook, stirring constantly, for a further 1 minute.

2. Leave to cool for 5 minutes, then gradually beat in the eggs and egg white to make a thick and glossy paste.

3. Line a baking sheet with baking paper. Spoon the paste into a large piping bag fitted with a large star nozzle and pipe eight 8-cm/3¼-inch rings of the paste onto the prepared baking sheet. Place in the freezer for 1 hour.

4. Heat enough oil for deep-frying in a large saucepan or deep-fryer to 180–190°C/350–375°F, or until a cube of bread browns in 30 seconds. Carefully remove the semi-frozen rings from the baking sheet, add to the hot oil in batches of 2–3 and fry on each side for 2–3 minutes, until crisp and deep golden brown. Remove with a slotted spoon and drain on kitchen paper.

5. To make the glaze, sift the icing sugar into a large bowl and beat in the milk until smooth. Dip the warm crullers in the glaze to coat completely and transfer to a wire rack to set.

Crisp and golden with a sweet, sticky glaze, these yeast-free doughnuts are very simple to make. They are best eaten within a few hours of making.

Baked Pumpkin
Doughnuts

MAKES	PREP	COOK
6	**25**	**15** MINUTES

INGREDIENTS

115 g/4 oz self-raising flour

½ tsp baking powder

½ tsp salt

1 tsp ground cinnamon

½ tsp grated nutmeg

50 g/1¾ oz butter, softened, plus extra for greasing

50 g/1¾ oz soft light brown sugar

1 large egg, beaten

1 tsp vanilla extract

1 tbsp milk

115 g/4 oz canned pumpkin purée

GLAZE

115 g/4 oz icing sugar

½ tsp ground cinnamon

2 tbsp milk

1–2 tsp maple syrup

1. Preheat the oven to 190°C/375°F/Gas Mark 5. Grease a 6-hole doughnut tin.

2. Sift together the flour and baking powder into a bowl and stir in the salt, cinnamon and nutmeg. Put the butter and brown sugar into a separate bowl and beat together until pale and creamy. Gradually beat in the egg, vanilla extract and milk. Fold in the flour mixture and pumpkin purée.

3. Spoon the mixture into a large piping bag fitted with a plain nozzle and pipe into the prepared tin. Bake in the preheated oven for 15 minutes, until risen, golden and just firm to the touch. Leave to cool for 5 minutes, then turn out onto a wire rack to cool completely.

4. To make the glaze, sift together the icing sugar and cinnamon into a bowl, add the milk and maple syrup and stir until smooth. Dip the top of each doughnut in the glaze and leave to set.

Smooth pumpkin purée gives these light baked doughnuts a lovely colour and delicious moist texture. For a spicier flavour use ground ginger instead of nutmeg.

Mocha Beignets

MAKES **PREP** **COOK**
24 **40** **20** MINUTES
PLUS RISING

INGREDIENTS

5 tbsp hot strong black coffee

40 g/1½ oz soft light brown sugar

1½ tsp easy-blend dried yeast

¼ tsp salt

1 egg, beaten

125 ml/4 fl oz evaporated milk, warmed

350 g/12 oz strong white flour, plus extra for dusting and kneading

25 g/1 oz white vegetable fat, softened

oil, for deep-frying

2 tbsp finely chopped plain chocolate

GLAZE

115 g/4 oz icing sugar

1 tbsp cocoa powder

1 tbsp cold strong black coffee

1–2 tbsp milk

1. Place the coffee in a large bowl and whisk in the sugar until dissolved. Leave to cool for 5 minutes, then whisk in the yeast, salt, egg and evaporated milk. Stir in half the flour and mix to a smooth batter. Beat in the vegetable fat. Add the remaining flour and mix to a soft dough.

2. Turn out the dough onto a lightly floured surface and knead for 4–5 minutes, until smooth and elastic, adding a little more flour if needed. Place the dough in a bowl, cover and leave in a warm place for about 2 hours, or until doubled in size.

3. Heat enough oil for deep-frying in a large saucepan or deep-fryer to 180–190°C/350–375°F, or until a cube of bread browns in 30 seconds.

4. Meanwhile, knock back the dough and roll out on a lightly floured surface to a thickness of 8 mm/⅜ inch. Use a 5-cm/2-inch round cookie cutter to stamp out 24 rounds, re-kneading and rolling the trimmings once.

5. Add the rounds, about 4 at a time, to the hot oil and fry on each side for 1–2 minutes, or until puffed up and deep golden brown. Baste the top of the beignets by gently spooning hot oil over them – this will help them to puff up. Remove with a slotted spoon and drain on kitchen paper.

6. To make the glaze, sift together the icing sugar and cocoa powder into a bowl and stir in the coffee and enough milk to make a smooth glaze. Dip each warm beignet in the glaze and sprinkle with chopped chocolate. Serve immediately.

You can make the dough for these doughnuts the night before and leave it to rise slowly in the refrigerator overnight, ready to fry in the morning.

Boston Cream Doughnuts

MAKES **12** PREP **45** COOK **20** MINUTES

PLUS RISING

INGREDIENTS

175 ml/6 fl oz milk

25 g/1 oz butter

350 g/12 oz strong white flour, plus extra for dusting and kneading

½ tsp salt

25 g/1 oz caster sugar

1½ tsp easy-blend dried yeast

1 egg, beaten

oil, for deep-frying and greasing

4 tbsp vanilla custard

100 ml/3½ fl oz double cream, lightly whipped

GLAZE

100 g/3½ oz plain chocolate, finely chopped

100 ml/3½ fl oz double cream

---

1. Put the milk and butter into a small saucepan over a low heat and heat until the butter has melted. Leave to cool for 5 minutes.

2. Sift the flour into a large bowl and stir in the salt, sugar and yeast. Pour in the milk mixture and the egg and mix to a soft dough. Turn out the dough onto a floured surface and knead for 5–6 minutes, until smooth and elastic, adding a little more flour if needed.

3. Place the dough in a bowl, cover and leave in a warm place for 1 hour or until doubled in size. Line a large baking sheet with baking paper.

4. Knock back the dough, divide into 12 pieces and roll each piece into a ball. Flatten slightly, place on the prepared baking sheet and cover with lightly oiled clingfilm. Leave in a warm place for 10–15 minutes, until puffy.

5. Heat enough oil for deep-frying in a large saucepan or deep-fryer to 180–190°C/350–375°F, or until a cube of bread browns in 30 seconds. Add the doughnuts to the hot oil, 3–4 at a time, and fry on each side for 1–2 minutes, or until golden. Remove with a slotted spoon and drain on kitchen paper. Leave to cool.

6. Use the tip of a small knife to make a hole in the side of each doughnut. Push the blade a little way in and move from side to side to create a space. Fold the custard into the whipped cream, spoon into a piping bag with a plain nozzle and pipe into the centre of the doughnuts.

7. To make the glaze, put the chocolate into a heatproof bowl set over a saucepan of gently simmering water and heat until melted. Put the cream into a small saucepan over a medium heat and heat until almost boiling. Pour over the chocolate and stir until smooth. Leave to stand for 5 minutes, then dip the top of each doughnut in the glaze. Leave to set.

Based on the classic American layer cake, these rich doughnuts are filled with sweet vanilla cream and have a rich dark chocolate glaze.

Maple & Pecan Doughnuts

MAKES PREP COOK
6   45   15 MINUTES
PLUS RISING

INGREDIENTS

125 ml/4 fl oz milk

15 g/½ oz butter

3 tbsp maple syrup

275 g/9¾ oz strong white flour, plus extra for dusting and kneading

¼ tsp salt

1½ tsp easy-blend dried yeast

1 egg, beaten

oil, for deep-frying and greasing

25 g/1 oz pecan nuts, finely chopped

FROSTING

55 g/2 oz soft cheese

40 g/1½ oz icing sugar

1 tbsp maple syrup

1. Put the milk, butter and maple syrup into a small saucepan over a low heat and heat until the butter has melted. Leave to cool for 5 minutes.

2. Sift the flour into a large bowl and stir in the salt and yeast. Pour in the milk mixture and the egg and mix to a soft dough. Turn out the dough onto a floured surface and knead for 5–6 minutes, until smooth and elastic, adding a little more flour if needed. Place the dough in a bowl, cover and leave in a warm place for 1 hour, or until doubled in size. Line a large baking sheet with baking paper.

3. Knock back the dough and roll out on a lightly floured surface to a 15-x 30-cm/6-x 12-inch rectangle. Use a sharp knife to trim the edges then cut into 6 strips. Place on the prepared baking sheet and cover with lightly oiled clingfilm. Leave in a warm place for 10–15 minutes, until puffy.

4. Heat enough oil for deep-frying in a large saucepan or deep-fryer to 180–190°C/350–375°F, or until a cube of bread browns in 30 seconds. Add the doughnuts, 2–3 at a time, and fry on each side for 1–2 minutes, or until golden. Remove and drain on kitchen paper. Leave to cool.

5. To make the frosting, put the cheese into a bowl and beat with a wooden spoon until soft, then beat in the icing sugar and maple syrup until smooth. Spread the frosting over the tops of the doughnuts and sprinkle with the chopped nuts.

These Jumbo long doughnuts are perfect for sharing. For a quirky variation on the topping sprinkle with chopped crispy bacon instead of the pecan nuts.

Fudge Doughnuts

MAKES **8** PREP **45** COOK **25** MINUTES
PLUS RISING

INGREDIENTS

175 ml/6 fl oz milk

25 g/1 oz butter

350 g/12 oz strong white flour, plus extra for dusting and kneading

½ tsp salt

1½ tsp easy-blend yeast

25 g/1 oz caster sugar

1 egg, beaten

oil, for deep-frying and greasing

150 ml/5 fl oz double cream, whipped

FROSTING

55 g/2 oz butter

100 g/3½ oz soft light brown sugar

3 tbsp milk

1 tsp vanilla extract

70 g/2½ oz icing sugar, sifted

1. Put the milk and butter into a small saucepan over a low heat and heat until the butter has melted. Leave to cool for 5 minutes.

2. Sift the flour into a large bowl and stir in the salt, yeast and sugar. Pour in the milk mixture and the egg and mix to a soft dough. Turn out the dough onto a floured surface and knead for 5–6 minutes, until smooth and elastic, adding a little more flour if needed.

3. Put the dough into a bowl, cover and leave in a warm place for 1 hour, or until doubled in size. Line a large baking sheet with baking paper.

4. Knock back the dough, divide into 2 pieces and roll out each piece on a lightly floured surface to a 15-cm/6-inch square. Use a sharp knife to trim the edges, then cut each square into 4 smaller squares. Place on the prepared baking sheet and cover with lightly oiled clingfilm. Leave in a warm place for 10–15 minutes, until puffy.

5. Heat enough oil for deep-frying in a large saucepan or deep-fryer to 180–190°C/350–375°F, or until a cube of bread browns in 30 seconds. Add the doughnuts, 2–3 at a time, and fry on each side for 1–2 minutes, or until golden. Remove and drain on kitchen paper. Leave to cool.

6. Use the tip of a small knife to make a hole in the side of each doughnut. Push the blade a little way in and move from side to side to create a space. Spoon the whipped cream into a piping bag with a plain nozzle and pipe it into the centre of the doughnuts.

7. To make the frosting, put the butter and brown sugar into a saucepan over a medium heat and heat, stirring constantly, until the sugar has dissolved. Bring to the boil and boil for 1 minute, then stir in the milk and vanilla extract. Simmer for a further 1 minute, then stir in the icing sugar. Leave to cool for 10–20 minutes, until thickened. Dip each doughnut in the frosting and leave to set.

Popular as a sweet treat in Scotland these square doughnuts
have a whipped cream filling and a delicious, sticky,
vanilla-flavoured fudge frosting.

Soured Cream
Doughnuts

MAKES **24**   PREP **20**   COOK **40** MINUTES

INGREDIENTS

200 g/7 oz caster sugar

3 eggs

225 g/8 oz soured cream

1 tsp vanilla extract

450 g/1 lb plain flour,
plus extra for dusting
and kneading

1 tsp bicarbonate of soda

1 tsp baking powder

½ tsp salt

¼ tsp nutmeg

oil, for frying

GLAZE

200 g/7 oz icing sugar

3-4 tbsp water or milk

1. Beat the sugar and eggs together in a large bowl. Add the soured cream and vanilla extract. Mix well.

2. Add the dry ingredients and mix well again. Turn out onto a floured board and knead for 5 minutes. The dough should be fairly soft.

3. Roll out the dough to a 5 mm/¼ inch thickness. Use a floured doughnut cutter to stamp out 24 doughnuts.

4. Heat enough oil for deep-frying in a large saucepan or deep-fryer to 180-190°C/350-375°F, or until a cube of bread browns in 30 seconds. Cook the doughnuts, in batches, by dropping into the hot oil. Fry for 2 minutes or until golden brown. Remove with a slotted spoon and drain on kitchen paper.

5. To make the glaze, place the icing sugar in a bowl and slowly mix in the water or milk until smooth.

6. Pour the glaze over the cooled doughnuts.

This delightful recipe uses soured cream instead of milk, making them wonderfully light and moist.

Cream Cheese & Herb
Doughnuts

MAKES PREP COOK
16 45 20 MINUTES
PLUS RISING

INGREDIENTS

175 ml/6 fl oz milk

2 tbsp olive oil

350 g/12 oz strong white flour, plus extra for dusting and kneading

1 tsp salt

1½ tsp easy-blend dried yeast

25 g/1 oz finely grated Parmesan cheese

1 egg, beaten

oil, for deep-frying and greasing

FILLING

400 g/14 oz full-fat soft cheese

2 tbsp snipped fresh chives

2 tbsp finely chopped fresh parsley

salt and pepper

1. Put the milk and oil into a small saucepan over a low heat and heat until just lukewarm. Sift the flour into a large bowl and stir in the salt, yeast and Parmesan cheese. Pour in the milk mixture and egg and mix to a soft dough. Turn out the dough onto a floured surface and knead for 5–6 minutes, until smooth and elastic, adding a little more flour if needed.

2. Put the dough into a bowl, cover and leave in a warm place for 1 hour, or until doubled in size. Line two large baking sheets with baking paper.

3. Knock back the dough and roll out on a lightly floured surface to a 25-cm/10-inch square. Trim the edges with a sharp knife and cut into 16 small squares. Place on the prepared baking sheets and cover with lightly oiled clingfilm. Leave in a warm place for 10–15 minutes, until puffy.

4. Heat enough oil for deep-frying in a large saucepan or deep-fryer to 180–190°C/350–375°F, or until a cube of bread browns in 30 seconds. Add the doughnuts, 3–4 at a time, and fry on each side for 1–2 minutes, or until golden. Remove with a slotted spoon and drain on kitchen paper. Leave to cool.

5. To make the filling, beat together the cheese and herbs and season with salt and pepper. Slice the doughnuts in half horizontally and sandwich back together with the soft cheese filling.

These savoury doughnuts are great for a packed lunch or picnic. For a more luxurious filling add some slices of smoked salmon.

Cheese & Olive
Beignets

MAKES **32** PREP **25** COOK **25** MINUTES

INGREDIENTS

100 g/3½ oz unsalted butter, diced

300 ml/10 fl oz water

140 g/5 oz plain flour, sifted

½ tsp salt

2 large eggs, beaten

6 black olives, stoned and finely chopped

2 tbsp finely chopped fresh parsley

3 tbsp finely grated Parmesan cheese

oil, for deep-frying

sea salt flakes, for sprinkling

1. Put the butter and water into a large saucepan over a low heat and heat until the butter has melted. Bring to the boil, remove from the heat and tip in the flour and salt. Beat thoroughly until the mixture is smooth and comes away from the side of the pan. Leave to cool for 5 minutes, then gradually beat in the eggs to make a thick and glossy paste. Beat in the olives, parsley and 2 tablespoons of the cheese.

2. Heat enough oil for deep-frying in a large saucepan or deep-fryer to 180–190°C/350–375°F, or until a cube of bread browns in 30 seconds. Drop 6–8 walnut-sized spoonfuls of the mixture into the hot oil and fry, turning frequently, for 4–5 minutes, until crisp and deep golden brown. Remove with a slotted spoon and drain on kitchen paper. Keep warm while frying the remaining mixture.

3. Serve the beignets warm, sprinkled with the remaining cheese and the sea salt flakes.

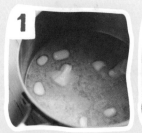

These light and crisp savoury
doughnuts are made with choux
pastry. Serve as a simple starter
or canapé.

Cornbread & Pepper

Doughnuts

MAKES **6**   PREP **20**   COOK **12** MINUTES

INGREDIENTS

15 g/½ oz butter, melted

1 tsp finely grated Parmesan cheese

70 g/2½ oz self-raising flour

1 tsp baking powder

85 g/3 oz fine cornmeal

½ tsp salt

¼ tsp pepper

1 large egg

6 tbsp buttermilk or natural yogurt

2 tbsp olive oil

1 spring onion, trimmed and very finely chopped

25 g/1 oz red pepper, deseeded and very finely chopped

1. Preheat the oven to 200°C/400°F/Gas Mark 6. Liberally brush the melted butter in the holes of a 6-hole doughnut tin, then sprinkle in the cheese.

2. Sift together the flour and baking powder into a large bowl and stir in the cornmeal and salt and pepper. Beat together the egg, buttermilk and oil and stir into the dry ingredients. Beat until smooth, then stir in the spring onion and red pepper.

3. Spoon the mixture into a piping bag fitted with a plain nozzle and pipe into the prepared tin. Bake in the preheated oven for 10–12 minutes, or until risen, golden and firm to the touch. Leave to cool in the tin for 2–3 minutes, then carefully loosen from the tin with a round-bladed knife. Serve immediately.

Perfect for serving at a weekend brunch, these savoury baked doughnuts are easy to prepare and take only minutes to make. They are best eaten warm from the oven.

Chilli & Chocolate
Churros

MAKES **16** PREP **20** COOK **25** MINUTES

INGREDIENTS

100 g/3½ oz unsalted butter, diced

225 ml/8 fl oz water

140 g/5 oz plain flour, sifted

large pinch of salt

2 large eggs, beaten

½ small red chilli, deseeded and very finely chopped

oil, for deep-frying

4 tbsp sugar

2 tsp cocoa powder, sifted

CHOCOLATE SAUCE

85 g/3 oz plain chocolate, broken into pieces

100 ml/3½ fl oz double cream

½ tsp vanilla extract

1 tsp dried chilli flakes, crushed

1. To make the chocolate sauce, put the chocolate and cream into a heatproof bowl set over a saucepan of gently simmering water and heat until the chocolate is melted. Remove from the heat and stir until smooth, then stir in the vanilla extract and chilli flakes. Set aside and keep warm.

2. Put the butter and water into a large saucepan over a low heat and heat until the butter has melted. Bring to the boil, remove from the heat and tip in the flour and salt. Beat thoroughly until the mixture is smooth and comes away from the side of the pan. Leave to cool for 5 minutes, then gradually beat in the eggs to make a thick and glossy paste. Beat in the chilli.

3. Heat enough oil for deep-frying in a large saucepan or deep-fryer to 180–190°C/350–375°F, or until a cube of bread browns in 30 seconds. Spoon the paste into a large piping bag fitted with a large star nozzle and pipe four 10-cm/4-inch lengths of the paste into the hot oil. Fry for 2–3 minutes, turning frequently, until crisp and golden. Remove with a slotted spoon and drain on kitchen paper. Keep warm while frying the remaining mixture.

4. Mix together the sugar and cocoa powder on a flat plate and toss the warm churros in the mixture to coat. Serve immediately with the chocolate sauce for dipping.

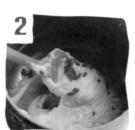

Chilli and chocolate make a surprisingly good flavour combination. So be adventurous and try these classic Mexican doughnuts.

Spiced Doughnut
Holes

MAKES **PREP** **COOK**
18 20 20 MINUTES
PLUS RESTING

INGREDIENTS

125 ml/4 fl oz milk, warmed
1 egg
2 tbsp natural yogurt
1 tsp vanilla extract
225 g/8 oz plain flour
2 tsp baking powder
½ tsp salt
70 g/2½ oz caster sugar, plus extra for dusting
1 tsp grated nutmeg
25 g/1 oz butter
oil, for greasing and frying

1. Mix together the warmed milk, egg, yogurt and vanilla extract in a bowl.

2. Using a stand mixer fitted with a paddle attachment, mix the flour, baking powder, salt, sugar and nutmeg together. Slowly add the butter and blend. Slowly add the milk mixture until the mixture is smooth and thick and resembles biscuit dough.

3. Leave the dough to rest in the mixer for 20 minutes.

4. Heat enough oil for deep-frying in a large saucepan or deep-fryer to 180-190°C/350-375°F, or until a cube of bread browns in 30 seconds. Drop the dough, 1 tablespoon at a time, into the hot oil. Fry for 1 minute or until golden brown. Remove with a slotted spoon and drain on kitchen paper.

5. Sprinkle with caster sugar and serve.

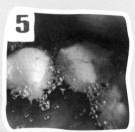

The nutmeg used in this recipe makes beautifully sweet and spicy doughnut holes — the perfect mini treat!

Vanilla, Cinnamon & Chocolate Doughnuts

MAKES 24 **PREP** 60 **COOK** 30 MINUTES
PLUS RISING

INGREDIENTS

300 g/10½ oz gluten-free, wheat-free flour blend

60 g/2¼ oz brown rice flour

¼ tsp xanthan gum

¼ tsp gluten-free baking powder

¼ tsp ground nutmeg

¼ tsp ground cinnamon

60 g/2¼ oz butter, softened

100 g/3½ oz ground almonds

½ tsp vanilla extract

1 egg plus 1 egg yolk

1 tbsp buttermilk

24 gluten-free dark chocolate buttons

150 g/5½ oz caster sugar, to dust

20 g/¾ oz ground cinnamon, to dust

oil, for greasing and frying

gluten-free chocolate sauce, to serve

YEAST MIX

10 g/¼ oz dried yeast

1½ tsp honey

1. To make the yeast mix, add 125 ml/4 fl oz tepid water to the dried yeast in a jug and stir in the honey. Leave to stand at room temperature for 15 minutes until frothy.

2. Sift the flours, xanthan gum, baking powder, nutmeg and cinnamon into a large bowl. Rub the butter into the flour mixture using your fingertips, until the mixture resembles fine breadcrumbs. Stir in the almonds, vanilla extract, egg, egg yolk and buttermilk. Pour in the yeast mix and stir well to form a dough, adding a little more water if required. Leave in a warm place until doubled in size.

3. Form 24 small dough balls and insert a chocolate button inside each one. Place them onto a baking tray covered in greased baking paper and cover with lightly greased clingfilm for 40 minutes.

4. Meanwhile, make the sugar dusting for the doughnuts by mixing the caster sugar and ground cinnamon together.

5. Heat enough oil to just cover the doughnuts in a large pan or deep-fryer to 180–190°C/350–375°F, or until a cube of bread browns in 30 seconds. Cook the doughnuts in the hot oil (3–4 at a time) for 2–3 minutes on each side until golden brown. Remove with a slotted spoon, drain on kitchen paper and roll in the sugar dusting. Serve with chocolate sauce.

These doughnuts are gluten- and wheat-free so are ideal to make for guests with these dietary requirements.

Cider Doughnuts

MAKES **12**   PREP **20**   COOK **35** MINUTES

INGREDIENTS

225 ml/8 fl oz sweet cider or apple juice

250 g/9 oz self-raising flour, plus extra for dusting

1½ tsp baking powder

1 tsp ground cinnamon

¼ tsp salt

55 g/2 oz soft light brown sugar

1 large egg, beaten

4 tbsp buttermilk

25 g/1 oz butter, melted and slightly cooled

oil, for deep-frying

55 g/2 oz granulated sugar

1. Pour the cider into a saucepan and bring to the boil. Boil for 10–15 minutes, until reduced to about 4 tablespoons of syrup. Leave to cool.

2. Sift together the flour, baking powder and half the cinnamon into a large bowl. Stir in the salt and brown sugar. Make a well in the centre.

3. Put the cider syrup, egg, buttermilk and butter into a jug, mix and pour into the well. Mix to a fairly firm dough, adding a little extra flour if the dough is too sticky to handle. Knead lightly until just smooth.

4. Divide the dough into 12 pieces and roll each piece into a ball. Flatten each ball in the palms of your hands to a thickness of 1 cm/½ inch.

5. Heat enough oil for deep-frying in a large saucepan or deep-fryer to 180–190°C/350–375°F, or until a cube of bread browns in 30 seconds. Add the doughnuts, 4 at a time, and fry, turning frequently, for 3–4 minutes, or until crisp and deep golden. Remove and drain on kitchen paper.

6. Mix together the granulated sugar and the remaining cinnamon in a shallow dish and roll each hot doughnut in the mixture to coat. Serve warm or cold.

You can also make this recipe into
ring-shaped doughnuts. Simply
roll out the dough, then use a
cutter to stamp out the rings.